By His Word

A Wake-up Call to America's Churches

John Filippi

with Bruce Malone

And God said, Let there be light: and there was light.   *Genesis 1:3*

In the beginning was the word, and the word was with God, and the word was God. The same was in the beginning with God. **All things were made by Him**; and without him was not any thing made that was made.   *John 1:1-3*

For this they willfully are ignorant of, that **by the word of God** the heavens were of old, and the earth standing out of water and in the water: Whereby the world that then was, being overflowed with water, perished.   *2 Peter 3:5-6*

Search for the Truth
Publications
3275 Monroe Road
Midland, MI 48642
SearchfortheTruth.net

By His Word

A Wake-up Call to
America's Churches

First Printing: May 2004

Library of Congress Control Number: 2004090015

ISBN: 0-9715911-2-1

Copyright 2004 by John Filippi and Bruce Malone

Cover design by Janell Robertson

All verses excerpted from the King James Bible

Illustrations by permission from Answers in Genesis, the Institute for Creation Research, and Chuck Asay

Dedication

This book is dedicated to the Reverend Carl W. Nelson and Charles A. Colberg of Gloria Dei Lutheran Church in Auburn Hills, Michigan; to my Christian brother Alvin, Commissiong of Hope Evangelical Lutheran Church in Citrus Springs, Florida, whose encouragement and printing of the first draft made this book possible; and to my wife and "sister in Christ", Vivian, whose patient support of the time involved and belief in its content enabled this work.

Acknowledgments

Thanks to the Institute for Creation Research and its founder, Henry M. Morris, for all of the material he has made available on this subject. We also wish to thank Answers In Genesis and its cofounder, Ken Ham, who resides in Florence, Kentucky and soon will have a world class creation museum located there. We truly appreciate permission from Christian brothers Dan Lietha (who was also born in Michigan's upper peninsula) and Chuck Asay for the extensive use of their insightful editorial illustrations. Thanks to Waino Tervo who helped immensely with both typing and revision of early manuscripts along with June Tervo, Darlene Hedin, and Anita O'Donnell who revised and corrected errors. Thanks also to Dr. Tas Walker, Steve Austin, Richard and Tina Kleiss, and Norma Powell for final revision suggestions before publication.

This book is a compilation of information gleamed from *Creation Magazine, Halley's Bible Handbook, The Bible Readers Companion* by L.O. Richards, *Christ Among Other Gods* by E.W. Lutzer, *Jesus Is Coming* by P.L. Tan, and *The Biblical Basis For Modern Science, Biblical Creationism & The Defender's Study Bible* by Dr. Henry M. Morris.

Contents

Foreword

America was started as a Christian nation. The buildings in Washington D.C. are covered with engravings of Scripture verses and Christian concepts. The three branches of government were set up as a balance of power in an attempt to restrict the sinful nature of mankind (a Judeo-Christian concept). The very design of our democratic republic is an effort to keep any group of sinful people from becoming dictatorial. Almost every original state constitution makes reference to God and/or Christianity. Yet our nation is rapidly losing its Christian foundation. Homosexual marriage is just around the corner and we can no longer acknowledge the Ten Commandments as the foundational basis for our laws. What is happening?

Throughout the last century our culture increasingly rejected the Bible as authoritative and replaced it with the opinions of men. This happened primarily because the historical statements of the Bible relating to the physical world – creation, the fall of mankind, and the global flood – have been denied as real events of history. If the people around you do not believe that these events are true, why should they believe the rest of the Bible is truth?

Christianity is, and always will be, at war with the lies of Satan. Satan seeks to *"devour us like a roaring lion"*[1] and comes into our lives to *"steal, kill, and destroy."*[2] He is the *"father of lies"*[3] and the greatest of his lies in our age is that the earth is billions of years old and that randomly guided processes such as evolution created us. We are told to *"love the Lord thy God with all thy heart, and with all thy soul, and with all thy mind, and with all thy strength."*[4] In other words we are to love God, morally, spiritually, intellectually, and physically.

Satan is busy destroying our nation morally (through sexually immorality and homosexuality), spiritually (by undermining belief in the Bible), intellectually (through the teaching of the bankrupt myth of evolution), physically (through abortion, euthanasia, drugs, alcohol, and increasing violent crime). What has been the Church's primary response through most of the twentieth century? *The Christian Church continues to fight the symptoms of moral decay while doing little to help people trust the source of moral truths (the Bible.)* If the church does not start connecting the Bible to the physical world around us, we will continue to lose both the moral battles and our culture. Even when fighting the symptoms of moral decay pastors seldom put any real emphasis on dealing with the root cause of this decay—the rejection of God's Word.

This book reveals the importance of acknowledging the literal straightforward understanding of the first eleven chapters of Genesis—which lay the foundation for every major Christian doctrine. There have been hundreds of books written on the scientific evidence supporting both a literal creation and a young earth. There are also hundreds of books exposing why evolution does not explain the world or its formation. Two excellent resources on these subjects can be found in the back of this book.

By His Word is not so much about the overwhelming evidence in favor of creation but the importance of trusting God's Word. The acknowledgment of a literal creation, a worldwide flood, and a young earth are THE KEY to reclaiming our Christian heritage.

To Jesus be the glory!

Bruce Malone

1. *1Peter 5:8*   2. *John 10:10*   3. *John 8:44*
4. *Mark 12:30*

Preface

I was at Cobo Hall in Detroit, Michigan in 1962 during the constituting convention of the Lutheran Church in America (LCA). At that time the Lutheran Church of the Finns, Swedes, Danes, Norwegians, and many others came together to form a unified body. Forty years ago the entire Lutheran church was teaching and preaching that all of God's Word could be trusted as written—in a straightforward manner.

Less than two decades later, in 1988, the LCA embraced other groups to form the Evangelical Lutheran Church in America (ELCA). Over the last two decades I have noticed an increasing trend toward liberalism* and the deviation from the inspired Word of God. My concern increased when the ELCA joined forces with a Lutheran group which had split off from the Lutheran Church Missouri Synod (LCMS). The Missouri Synod, to their credit, would take no part in liberalism of God's Word— which is why this group split from that part of the denomination.

As I observed our denomination deviating further and further from the truth of God's Word, I prayed to God for direction and guidance. I asked Him to use me to help return truth to our church. In response to this prayer I was led to the Institution for Creation Research (ICR), headed at that time by Henry M. Morris and now by his son John D. Morris. Through this acquaintance I also came to know and respect Ken Ham and his organization, Answers in Genesis (AIG). From these acquaintances I soon realized

---

* *Liberalism of God's Word is ignoring the clear straightforward statements of Scripture and reinterpreting these statements to mean something different than the message they were written to convey. (Exegesis to Eisegesis)*

what is taking place, not only in our church, but throughout Western society. Not only have we deviated from God's inspired Word, we have blended it with godless evolutionary philosophy.

Many Christians think that creation/evolution is an irrelevant side issue. However, creation forms the foundation from which we can effectively witness about our Lord Jesus Christ to our modern culture. People have become hardened to the reality that they need Jesus Christ as their Savior. They have been taught all of their lives that they are just highly evolved animals. Until we dispel this lie, we will not reach people with the relevance of who Jesus Christ is and why He came to Earth.

Creation is essential for showing our lost culture that God's Word is total truth — there is abundant physical evidence that backs up the Bible's historical, archaeological and geological claims. This is not true of any other religion in the world.

The information contained within *By His Word* is a brief summary of the lifelong work of many great saints of God. My part is merely compiling and rewording the information from others who have gone before me. I thank God for directing me to ICR and Henry M. Morris as well as AIG and Ken Ham. Both of these great men of God have opened my eyes to the need for creation evangelism. My wish is that the truth contained within these pages will be a blessing to you.

I humbly propose to my sisters and brothers in Christ that the information contained in this volume represents the most straightforward way of understanding the inspired Word of God. The Holy Bible is 100% true, and accurately describes the past, present, and the future.

John Filippi

8

Chapter 1:
It's Time to Teach the Truth

" If I profess every portion of the truth except that little point which the devil and the world are at that moment attacking, I am not professing Christ. For where the battle rages, there the loyalty of the soldier is proven. To be steady on all battlefields besides, is mere flight and disgrace, if he flinches at the point of fiercest attack."

-Martin Luther

The modern Christian Church faces a crisis as significant as it faced in 1517 when Martin Luther nailed his 95 theses on the door of the church in Wittenberg, Germany. Martin Luther observed that the church fathers were not teaching

Martin Luther Burning Indulgences

God's Word as clearly written. He wrote to his former teacher in Erfurt, Professor Jodokus Trutfetter, saying, *"I am firmly convinced that it is impossible to reform the church unless canons, decretals, scholastic theology, philosophy and logic, as they are now taught, are completely uprooted, and other subjects are taught. In addition, I go so far in the conviction, as to beg the Lord every day that the study of the Bible and the holy fathers may at once be restored in all its purity."*[1]

Our church is in the same situation today. There are two basic world views: the God-centered worldview (creation) and the man-centered worldview (evolution). When our church leaders try to combine these two views, we end up with a foundationless theology which blasphemes God's Word.

Throughout history man has demonstrated what happens when he sets the rules instead of obeying God's moral commands. The French Revolution of 1789 gives us the perfect example of a society started from a totally man-centered foundation. After the French revolutionaries threw out the aristocracy and church, the stage was set for men to declare that their rules, not God's, should control society. Unlike the American revolution which was firmly rooted in the biblical concept that *"all men are created equal, that they are endowed* **by their Creator** *with certain unalienable rights, that among these are life, liberty and the pursuit of happiness"*[2] the French Revolution was rooted in the "goodness of mankind", with human reason making just laws and determining right from wrong. This foundation did not result in freedom and justice but produced a bloodbath for innocent citizens, whose only crime was being in opposition to the philosophy of those in power. This violent birth of pure socialistic humanism was in stark contrast to the American Revolution, which was founded firmly upon the acknowledgment of God as Creator. During the French Revolution the opinions of those in control were forced upon others. Might became right. French philosopher Jean Jacques Rousseau (1712 - 1778) believed that people who did not agree with the majority should be forced to agree. In his words, they should be "forced to be free." Those who refused to be "free" were eliminated.

There are those today who hold similar views but just use different words. We are told by modern liberals that we must tolerate all views. In reality these liberals tolerate all views *except* those of the Christians who say we should obey God's law. Our society dictates that we should be *free* to abort children, *free* to be sexually active (even to the point of granting homosexuals special privileges), *free* to teach only evolution in public schools, and *free* to employ whom the government says you must employ. If you don't agree, the courts will *force* you to be free! In reality, Christian absolutes are being systematically eliminated from society. People today are anything but free.

The Bible, however, tells us what true freedom is: *"If ye continue in my word, then are ye my disciples indeed; and ye shall know the truth, and the truth shall make you free."*[3] True freedom is knowing where you came from, who owns you, what is wrong with you, and having

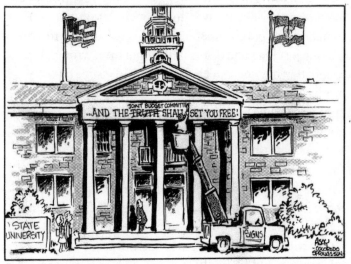

the solution to your sin dilemma. Rousseau's freedom, like that of many people today, is actually a bondage, a bondage to sin and its consequences. Examples of sin's consequences are AIDS and dozens of other sexually transmitted diseases. These diseases are the result of *not* obeying God's rules about sex. Thus, sexual "freedom" results in the bondage of sickness. The world is being led astray by a lie. Far from becoming more and more free, the world is falling deeper into the slavery of sin and its consequences, ignoring the real foundation upon which freedom is founded. Evolution is being used to lead people away from the truth of the Bible by undermining their confidence in the Bible's foundation. This foundation starts with the first eleven chapters of Genesis—our creation foundation.[4]

Many pastors of the Evangelical Lutheran Church in America (and other churches) are making the defense of God's Word (starting in Genesis) a priority in their churches. I am certain the Lord is blessing their work and bringing souls into the kingdom through these efforts. True believers within the church must do everything they can to support these courageous pastors in representing the truth. Consider putting creation resources to use in your own church. Everyone from elementary school students to grandparents can make a difference in our world by sharing the truth that God is our literal Creator and that the Bible can be trusted in every statement it makes—including statements about biology, geology, cosmology and history.

My own church belongs to the Florida-Bahamas Synod of the Evangelical Lutheran Church in America. It is my desire that a reformation would start within the ELCA, much like the reformation 500 years ago. At that time Martin Luther nailed a notice on the church door in an effort to bring the church back to trusting and teaching only God's Word. It is only "By His Word" that we can know the truth. We need to nail a *Literal Genesis Understanding Proclamation* to the symbolic door of every church in America. The following is such a resolution made to our church in Citrus Springs, Florida:

"Whereas, by starting a literal Genesis teaching ministry, people can be helped to understand that the creation/ evolution issue is not just about ape-man, fossils, the age of the earth and natural selection. All foundational issues for our faith must start with the acknowledgment that the Word of God is infallible, whereas the opinions of sinful humans are fallible. A Genesis ministry will help reestablish the foundation of the Word of God in our nation, which has been eroded and replaced in many areas by the teaching of evolution... Therefore, be it resolved that the Florida-Bahamas Synod of the ELCA will begin a program in the teaching of a Genesis ministry to restore the creation foundation to our churches and to our nation."[5]

1. *Luther: An Introduction to His Thought*, Gerhard Ebeling, Chapter 1, p.19.
2. *The American Declaration of Independence*
3. *John 8:31-32*
4. *Genesis and the Decay of the Nations*, Ken Ham Chapter 6, p.50, 51.
5. *Northern Great Lakes Synod Directory 1996 Assembly Minutes Resolution Number 13 SA95.05.18*, p. 115-116, John E. and Vivian D. Filippi, Hope Evangelical Lutheran Church, Citrus Springs, Fl.

Chapter 2:

The Need for Creation Evangelism

" The philosophy of the school room in one generation will be the philosophy of government in the next."

- Abraham Lincoln

" The Bible...contains an immense amount of evidence as to its authenticity...let us treat the Bible fairly. If we had a witness on the stand whose general story was true, we would believe him even when he asserted the facts of which we have no other evidence. We ought to treat the Bible with equal fairness. I decided long ago that it was less difficult to believe that the Bible was what it claimed to be than to disbelieve it. "

- Abraham Lincoln

Many people refuse to acknowledge the evidence that the Bible is the inspired Word of God because to do so challenges their long-held position that the Bible cannot be literally trusted. Once someone is trained to believe that they cannot trust the Bible, and they begin to view life from an agnostic perspective, it becomes very hard for them to admit that they are wrong. Those who have rejected God and the Bible have a huge emotional and intellectual investment in their agnosticism.

Others refuse to submit to the truth of the Word of God because they fear the changes in daily life, habits and priorities that the Word of God may bring them to make. When faced with evidence that the Bible is truly inspired by God, these people feel threatened because they must now think seriously about their responsibility to God. Since they have never known God personally, they do not understand the blessings which come from such a relationship (such as finding meaning in life which does not depend on power, possessions, people or health; the confidence that comes from being loved unconditionally; and the total removal of the fear of death).

Still others have never seriously considered the claims of Jesus Christ to be Creator, Savior and Lord. Their casual denial of the authority of the Bible has shielded them from tough questions such as: What if the Bible is true? What if there is a heaven, a hell and the possibility of eternal separation from God? Where will I spend eternity? How can I be assured that I will go to heaven?

Many in our modern, religiously pluralistic society are offended by the Bible's declaration that there is only one possible way to be saved, but the apostle Peter spoke clearly about the absolute necessity of faith in Jesus Christ alone. *"[Only by the name of Jesus Christ]...Neither is there salvation in any other: for there is no other name under heaven given among men whereby we must be saved."*[1]

Many people would like to believe that as long as they are sincere and live a reasonably good life, they will make it to heaven. This is a lie from the pit of hell. The Word of

AFTER EDEN
by Dan Lietha

www.AnswersInGenesis.org

I HAVEN'T SINNED TOO MUCH. I'M SURE GOD WILL LET ME INTO HEAVEN.

ARE YOU SURE? ARE YOU AS GOOD AS ADAM AND EVE WERE BEFORE THEY EXCEEDED THE 'SIN LIMIT' AND GOD KICKED THEM OUT OF EDEN?

© 2001 AiG

BUT THEY ONLY SINNED **ONCE** AND WERE KICKED OUT OF EDEN!

THE SAME GOD MADE HEAVEN. STILL THINK YOU'RE GETTING IN?

DAN LIETHA

Romans 3:23

Used by permission of AiG - www.AnswersInGenesis.org

God declares that sincerity is not enough. If you are sincere in your faith, but choose to reject Jesus Christ, you have placed your faith in your own actions rather than God's grace. You may be totally sincere, but you are still sincerely wrong, because you have rejected Christ's sacrificial death for your salvation. Without this the Bible clearly teaches that you are lost for eternity. The sole entrance requirement into heaven is your faith relationship to Jesus Christ. The sacrificial gift of His life paid the price for our sins. Only by accepting His pardon can we stand before the judgment seat of God clothed in Christ's righteousness.

The gospel of Jesus Christ does not begin in the New Testament. It begins in the very first chapter of Genesis. Once people understand that the Bible can be trusted, they become open to what it says about their sin nature. Jesus himself stated, *"If I have told you earthly things and ye believe not, how shall ye believe, if I tell you of heavenly things?"*[2] This is a key verse if we are to understand why Europe has become essentially anti-Christian over the last century and America is rapidly heading in the same direction.

In order to bring people to understand the relevance of the Bible and Jesus Christ in our modern, technology-driven world, we must first help them understand that the Bible can be trusted when it speaks about our physical world. They need to understand that the Bible is correct when it tells us where everything came from and why it functions the way that it does. If the Bible cannot be trusted when it speaks about biology (each creature reproduces after its own kind); geology (there has been a global flood that produced the fossil record); and, the nature of mankind (sin and death are a result of man's actions)—then why should anyone trust its spiritual and moral claims?

1. *Acts 4:10-12*
2. *John 3:12*

Section 1 - Theological Jello™

If you tried to nail Jello to the wall you would find that it oozes off and falls to the floor. Sadly, when it comes to the book of Genesis, many church leaders—even conservative Christian leaders—treat the Word of God like nothing more than what Ken Ham calls, "theological jello."[1] In other words, they do not accept what it says but mold God's Word to fit the ever changing shape of the latest *"scientific"* speculation.

The Bible should be understood as real history—in the same way that Jesus and Paul understood it when quoting Genesis. It's obvious that the text of Genesis means to convey the message that God created the earth in six ordinary days, and that the earth cannot be billions of years old. In spite of this, these same church leaders insist that we must accept the billions of years for the age of the earth (which they call science), and reinterpret Genesis to fit this "scientific interpretation." However, if we use science to reinterpret the Word of God in Genesis, why not use science to reinterpret the resurrection of Jesus? If these leaders are consistent, they have to reject the bodily resurrection of Christ and the virgin birth. After all, science regards such events as impossible.

The reason we believe in the bodily resurrection of Christ and the virgin birth is *because of the words of Scripture*. And the reason we should believe in six days of creation is also *because of the words of Scripture*. Furthermore, there is abundant scientific evidence to support this claim of a young earth. A belief in a literal six day creation simply takes Scripture at face value, as clearly written, rather than reinterpreting it to fit atheistic philosophy.

We will never be in error if we judge man's theories according to Scripture rather than Scripture according to man's theories. If man's ideas don't line up with the clear teaching of Scripture, then they should be discarded because history and science has shown that they will invariably be wrong. Church leaders should be teaching their congregations to trust the straightforward teaching of Scripture. Sadly, this is not happening in most churches today.

A recent Baker Book House publication, *The Baker Encyclopedia of Christian Apologetics*, authored by the Christian scholar and theologian, Norman Geisler, is an example of the muddled thinking of many church leaders in this area. This book was written to help Christians defend their faith, but in the important area of creation it does the opposite. It is pitiful to read the theological jello in this resource as it undermines what the book of Genesis actually says. Yet once the author moves on to other books of the Bible he provides an excellent model for apologetics.

The Baker Encyclopedia of Christian Apologetics is typical of much that is coming out of Christian circles today; applying one method of interpretation to Genesis and another to the rest of the Bible. For instance, the author admits that *"there is **prima facie** evidence to indicate the days of Genesis 1 are indeed twenty-four hour periods."* However, he then lists all the supposed "scientific" problems with this viewpoint. Dr. Geisler concludes with: *"If, of course, the days of Genesis are long periods of time, then there is no conflict with modern science on the age of the earth. But, even if the days of Genesis are twenty-four hours, there are still ways to reconcile long periods of time with Genesis chapters 1-2."* After reading this section you really don't know what to believe, except that the author has no idea what to believe. Pure theological jello!

When you read Dr. Geisler's section on the resurrection, he again gives numerous arguments for and against this

Recipe for Theological Jello

Mix God's perfect, unchanging Word
with man's fallible, ever-changing opinions.

WARNING: You cannot stand
on Theological Jello.

©AIG 2000

event. He concludes by stating that ultimately God's Word
must be trusted because God's Word clearly teaches a
bodily resurrection of Christ. The reader is told in no
uncertain terms that one must accept the bodily resurrection
of Christ.

The inconsistency of such theology is glaring. The
majority of Christian leaders reject six literal days of
creation because they are willing to accept the word of
atheistic scientists, who only present data from those few
methods that indicate an earth old enough to allow for
evolution. Yet church leaders insist on the literal resurrection
of Christ when these same scientists would insist that this is
scientifically impossible.

The real issue is whether we are willing to take God at
His Word and use Scripture to judge the fallible theories of
sinful man —or whether we will use the fallible theories of
man to judge the infallible Word of God. *"Every word of*

God is pure; He is a shield unto them who put their trust in Him. Add thou not unto His words, lest He reprove thee, and thou be found a liar."[2]

Let's be consistent in how we take God's Word. We need to let God speak to us through the words of Scripture. To the best of our ability, we should not impose ideas from *outside* the Bible on the Word of God. To do so is to make fallible, sinful man the authority over God.

AFTER EDEN
by Dan Lietha

Gap theory

Day-age theory

www.AnswersInGenesis.org

Theistic evolution

Genesis 3:1

© 2003 AiG

Used by permission of AiG - www.AnswersInGenesis.org

In the beginning, the serpent in Eden was 'crafty' with God's Word. Since then, we've been crafty too.

All Christians acknowledge that the bodily resurrection of Jesus Christ is an essential part of the gospel, *"If Christ be not raised your faith is in vain"[3]*, yet they do not understand that believing in a literal six day creation is just as critical to the gospel message. Think about the implications. As soon as one accepts huge periods of earth history, one must logically also accept millions of years of

Jesus Christ, who repeatedly claimed to be God, clearly recognized and understood Genesis to be literal and true.

death, bloodshed, disease, thorns, and suffering in the fossil record before man's existence. If these things existed before sin, the very reason for Jesus' death becomes irrelevant. If death occurred for millions of years before sin, then why should death have anything to do with the result of our sins? How do we know for sure that Jesus' sacrifice on the cross was payment for our sins?

Jesus frequently quoted from the writings of Moses and the book of Genesis. When questioned about marriage He referred to the literal creation of Adam and Eve.[4] When asked about the timing of His second coming, He said it would be when the conditions on the earth were similar to the apathetic (and sinful) conditions of the world before the literal worldwide flood occurred.[5] When accused of breaking sabbath laws, He referred to the fourth commandment which states that God made the entire universe in six literal days.[6] Jesus Christ, who repeatedly claimed to be God, clearly recognized and understood

Genesis to be literal and true. He couldn't have made this any more clear when He stated that, *"If they hear not Moses and the prophets, neither will they be persuaded, though one rose from the dead."*[7]

Rejecting the six literal days of creation not only undermines the authority of Scripture, but it also undermines the good news of Jesus Christ. This is one of the primary reasons that so many people find Christianity irrelevant to their lives today.[1]

1. *Creation Magazine*, Vol.7, no.3, March 2000, Ken Ham, AiG Ministries, Florence, KY.
2. *Proverbs 30:5-6*
3. *1 Corinthians 15:17*
4. *Matthew 19:3-6*
5. *Matthew 24:37-39*
6. *Exodus 20:9-11*
7. *Luke 16:31*

Section 2 - The Bible and the Earth's Age

At the center of the evolution/creation controversy is the question of the age of the earth. Just what does the Bible tell us concerning the age of the earth? In Genesis chapter 1 the Bible clearly indicates that the entire universe was created in six literal days (a day being defined in the very first chapter of Genesis as one rotation of the earth). The text makes this exceedingly clear, by stating that each day had a morning and an evening. Furthermore, the days are numbered to make it undeniable that literal sequential days are intended by the author. To make more certain that mankind could not misunderstand the meaning of "day", the only one of the ten commandments with a justification ties the commandment to the creation of the universe in six literal days, *"Remember the sabbath day to keep it holy...For in six days the LORD made heaven and earth, the sea, and all that is in them, and rested on the seventh day: wherefore the Lord blessed the sabbath day and hallowed it."*[1]

It is hard to imagine any way in which God could have made the meaning of how long He took to create the universe more apparent. It is only by refusing to believe what the Bible says, that anyone could come to the conclusion that God formed the universe and life over billions of years. God's Word clearly teaches otherwise.

As shown in the table on the next page, the amount of time which has passed since this six-day creation of the universe is also clearly taught by Scripture.[2] The age of each generation given in the early chapters of Genesis can be used to calculate the time elapsed from creation to the Flood, and from the Flood until the birth of Abraham. Later Bible verses can be used to determine the time which elapsed from the birth of Abraham until the time of Solomon

Name	Year of Birth	Age at Birth of Son	Age at Death	Year of Death[2]
Adam	0	130	930	930
Seth	130	105	912	1042
Enos	235	90	905	1140
Cainan	325	70	910	1235
Mahalaleel	395	65	895	1290
Jared	460	162	962	1422
Enoch	622	65	365[3]	987[4]
Methuselah	687	187	969	1656
Lamech	874	182	777	1651
Noah	1056	502	950	2006
Shem	1558	100	600	2158
Arphaxad	1658	35	438	2096
Salah	1693	30	433	2126
Eber	1723	34	464	2187
Peleg	1757	30	239	1996
Reu	1787	32	239	2026
Serug	1819	30	230	2049
Nahor	1849	29	148	1997
Terah	1878	70	205	2083
Abraham	1948	100	175	2123
Isaac	2048	60	180	2228
Jacob	2108	–	147	2255

Table 1 - Life Span of the Patriarchs

(1 Kings 6:1). More recent historical events and records clearly document how much time has elapsed since then.

There are several versions of the original Old Testament manuscripts and they agree an amazing 99% of the time. One of the astounding discoveries of the 2500 year old Dead Sea Scrolls is their almost total agreement with modern Bible manuscripts. Only minor variations are found. One of these minor variations involve the ages of the first ten generations from Adam to Noah. According to the ages in the Samaritan Pentateuch there were 1307 years from Adam to the Flood. According to the Masoretic text, which is generally considered to be the most reliable, there were 1656 years from Adam to the Flood. The Septuagint yields approximately 2300 years. Josephus, an ancient Jewish historian, used the Septuagint text to calculate the time from Adam to the Flood to be 2262 years.

	Elapsed Time	
Event	Minimum	Maximum
Creation to the Flood	1307	2402
Flood to Abraham	292	1513
Abraham to Christ	2000	2000
Christ to today	2004	2004
Total	5603	7919

Table 2 - Variation in Biblical Chronology

This information, including the disputed uncertainty, is summarized in the table 2. According to the highly regarded Massoetic text, the age of the earth is about 6000 years. However, even considering the variations between texts, the differences are relatively small. Thus, Scripture clearly indicates the age of the earth is between 5600-8000 years.

God often uses patterns in teaching us truth and history. There are many patterns within the Old Testament which foretold of the coming and purpose of Jesus. For example, the slaying of an innocent lamb as payment for the ancient Israelite sins was a pattern for the slaying of an innocent man—Jesus—as payment for our sins. It is an intriguing possibility that, just as the Bible indicates there were six days of creation followed by one day of rest, all of history may involve six thousand years of history followed by a thousand year reign of Christ (rest). As we have seen, the most reliable manuscripts put the time from creation to the present day at almost 6000 years. The return of Christ may be immanent indeed!

Regardless of the exact age of the earth, a billion-year old earth is out of the question. *A Closer Look at the Evidence* and *Search for the Truth* are both excellent resources for learning more about the vast majority of dating methods which indicate that the earth and universe are quite young. Order forms for both of these excellent resources may be found at the back of this book and at www.searchforthetruth.net.

In addition to the majority of dating methods which indicate that the earth is NOT billions of years old, belief in evolution contradicts the most basic laws of science. The first law of thermodynamics tells us that neither matter nor energy can create itself. This is in total agreement with Genesis chapter 2:1-3, which tells us that none of the tremendous energy of our universe is presently being created. Since the matter and energy in the universe could not have created itself, this law of science points to our Creator.

The question, which is essentially ignored by modern science: " Where did all of this heat, matter, energy and ordered complexity, come from in the first place" ?

The second law of thermodynamics states that the available (usable) energy of our universe is decreasing. This is in accordance with Romans 8:20-22 and Genesis 3:17-19, which both indicate that things are winding down. Therefore, sometime in the past, the total originally created energy had to have been in a more available form, like a clock that had just been wound. Thus, the second law also indicates that the universe was created and did not create itself. Another way of looking at the second law of thermodynamics is that heat always flows from hot to cold. Given enough time, everything in the universe will reach a uniform low temperature in which no processes, including life, are possible. This is commonly referred to as the "heat death" of the universe. The question which is essentially ignored by modern science is, "Where did all of the heat,

and ordered complexity, come from in the first place"?
Creation gives a reason and a source for this original more
highly ordered state (God and creation), whereas evolution
relies on faith in some yet to be determined scientific
mechanism to explain where all this more available energy
and original matter came from. Thus, both of these most
basic laws of science point inexorably back to Genesis
chapter one verse one— *"In the beginning God created
the heavens and the earth."*

It other words, the two laws of thermodynamics point to
an original time of creation when the total energy was both
created and ordered—the opposite of evolution which
would have us believe that less ordered matter became
more ordered and organized on its own.

1. *Exodus 20:8,11*
2. *The Defender's Bible,* Henry Morris, 1995, p.1544.

Section 3 - A Comparison of Religions

All religions and all worldviews attempt to answer the most basic questions of life. These questions include: Where did we come from? Why are we here? Why is the world the way it is? If we believe that we are the result of random evolutionary processes (such as mutations), we will come to a very different answer to these important questions than we would if we are the result of the direct creation by a loving God. The vast majority of the world's religions and philosophic worldviews have their foundation in evolution. This is a partial listing of those worldviews that are structured around the evolutionary philosophy:

Animism	Atheism	Bahaism
Behaviorism	Buddhism	Communism
Confucianism	Darwinism	Facism
Hinduism	Humanism	Jainism
Liberal Christianity	Liberal Islam	Liberal Judaism
Marxism	Mysticism	Nazism
New Age Religions	Occultism	Pantheism
Racism	Satanism	Shintoism
Sikhism	Spiritism	Socialism
Taoism	Unitarianism	

All of these anti-creation religions have adopted or have been founded on some variation of evolutionary thought. Many add good works as a way to earn favor with God. Those based purely on evolution are forced to believe that mankind must determine his own reality, deciding for himself what is right and wrong, depending on the situation at any given moment. This dependence on situational ethics is exactly what leads to corporate and political scandals.

There are only three religions which believe in a single creator God—Judaism, Islam and Christianity. These three religions are founded upon the acknowledgment of one self-existent eternal creator who called the universe into existence in the beginning, as well as both its physical and moral laws.

Out of these three creationist religions, only Orthodox Christianity shows that it is God who has provided a pathway to God's eternal kingdom that does not depend upon mankind's moral performance. Only Christianity reveals that God—through the sacrifice of Himself as Jesus Christ—makes a way for eternal peace with Himself. The gift of eternal life is freely given to anyone who willingly gives his life to the Lord Jesus Christ. This isn't the end of our spiritual journey but the beginning.

Jesus commanded us to make the truth of who He is known to all mankind. This must start by clearing away the lies of evolution which cloud the minds of so many, making them resistant to the truths of the Bible. All other religious beliefs attempt to bring peace and meaning through the work and actions of mankind. In essence, it is man who earns salvation, rather than God who gives it. In which case, who is really God?

Section 4 - Our Creation: Spirit, Soul, & Body

God created mankind quite different from any other creature. Throughout Scripture God describes Himself as threefold in nature and reveals Himself as Creator God, Spirit, and Savior Son. Although there is some disagreement as to whether mankind displays a dual or trinitary nature, the fact that we are made in the image of God would support the idea that we also display a threefold nature. With this assumption in mind, lets examine the nature of these three parts of our existence.

It seems to be our spirit which gives us **God-consciousness,** allowing us to sense and interact with God most directly. Our soul seems to be synonymous with our personality and mind. It is our soul which gives us **self-consciousness.** There is no disputing that it is our body and our senses which come into contact with the material world that gives us **world-consciousness**.

The order of importance and priority which we are to give to things is the same importance which God has always insisted upon:

- **First the Spirit**
- **Then the Soul**
- **Lastly the Body**

Without giving ourselves to Jesus Christ, the relative order of importance which we give to the individual components that make up who we are become reversed. Our bodies take preeminence over our spirit. A look at our decadent culture reveals that looks, sex, and health are gods of this age. Worship of the body has replaced spiritual worship. In a similar way, seeking some sort of spiritual enlightenment, followers of pagan religions emphasize the body by cutting themselves in an effort to gain favor with God. Our spiritual relationship with our Creator must always come first if we are to achieve the fulfillment we were designed to have. When God first created man he formed him of dust from the ground and then breathed "*The breath of life*"[1] into his nostrils. This very breath may have became man's spirit as it entered man's body and Adam became a living being, made in the image of his Creator. The following are good definitions of the three distinctly different parts which make up who we are.

The Spirit - This is the force that transmits its thoughts to the soul causing the soul to move the body to obey the spirit's orders.

The Soul - This is the site of man or woman's personality and influence. Prior to sin our souls were completely in one accord with God's Spirit.

The Body - This is the fleshly temple which nurtures and holds the soul while it is being developed for the hereafter.

Only the soul and the spirit are eternal. They will reside forever, either with or without their Creator. In the new creation we are promised a glorified body without pain or disease and we will spend eternity with our Creator. Without forgiveness of our current rebellion against the Lord we will live for eternity without our Creator in ultimate loneliness and despair. This is hell.

The soul has been characterized by a variety of names such as our will, mind, intellect and emotion. The soul is capable of loving, hating, desiring, aspiring, feeling and sensing. The soul actually is the very life of man and woman. Our body and soul are the place where our spirits reside. Neither God nor the devil can do any work without first obtaining our consent through our soul, since men and women have free wills.

Under normal conditions (without drugs etc.) the spirit is like the owner, the soul like the manager, and the body like the worker. The owner commands or commits matters to the manager who in turn commands the worker to carry them out. The owner (spirit) gives orders privately to the manager (soul); the manager (soul) transmits them openly to the worker (body). The manager (soul) appears to be lord of all, but in actuality the lord over all is the owner (spirit). Sin takes place when the proper order of spirit, soul, and body has been confused by Satan. This started approximately 6000 years ago in the Garden of Eden.

Satan has reversed God's order of spirit, soul and body through his temptations—initially, to the body (tempting Eve with food), then to the soul (appealing to the intellect with the knowledge of good and evil) and, lastly, to the spirit (offering for Eve to "be like God"). Satan continues to use these same techniques in various forms today.[2]

1. *Genesis 2:7*
2. *The Spiritual Man*, Chapter 1: Spirit, Soul and Body, Watchman Nee, Christian Fellowship Publishers, Inc., New York.

Chapter 3:
The Seven "C's" of Creation Evangelism

" The Bible is worth more than all other
books that have ever been printed."

- Patrick Henry

" It cannot be emphasized too strongly or
too often that this great nation was
founded, not by religionists, but by
Christians; not on religions, but on the
Gospel of Jesus Christ. For this very
reason peoples of other faiths have
been afforded asylum, prosperity, and
freedom of worship here."

- Patrick Henry

The Bible is irrelevant to many people because they do not believe it relates to the real world. They do not understand that it reveals the true history of the past, and they have been trained to believe that everything can be explained without God. Nothing could be further from the

To effectively reach people who consider the Bible irrelevant, we must first help them to realize that the Bible is true.

truth. To effectively reach people who consider the Bible irrelevant, we must first help them realize that the Bible is true. Creation evangelism lays the foundation to understand who Christ is by first explaining why He came.

Our public educational system and the media vehemently oppose any teaching of creation, a worldwide Flood and a young earth because it undermines the philosophic worldview which currently dominates these areas. Our educational system is controlled by a humanist philosophy which believes that mankind is basically good and that we can determine for itself what is right and wrong based on majority opinion and situational ethics. This is the logical conclusion if we have evolved over long periods of time. It is only by helping people understand that the Creation, the Fall of man and the Flood are reality, that they often become open to hearing the Gospel. These events form the very basis upon which true Christianity is built. Christianity can be summed up by the seven "C's" of history. Once these historical events are acknowledged, people begin to comprehend the real God. Often for the first time they understand how Christianity relates to the "real" physical world and begin to understand why things are the way they are. A true commitment to Jesus Christ is the logical next step. The seven "C's" of understanding the "real world" are essential if we are to bring people to a saving knowledge of Jesus Christ and return our country to its Christian foundation. The Bible clearly states that the following events form the framework to understand all of history:

CREATION - God created the universe in six literal twenty-four hour days, and when He had finished, He called His creation very good. The "first Adam" was literally created at this time. Adam was not the product of some mutated apelike creature.

CORRUPTION - God walked daily with Adam and Eve in the Garden of Eden until they disobeyed Him—causing a separation from God. This also brought death, struggle, and sin into God's very good creation.

CATASTROPHE - Because of the increasing and total wickedness of man on earth, God totally flooded planet earth and only those land animals (and humans) which were aboard Noah's Ark were saved.

CONFUSION - Again, due to human sin at the tower of Babel, God intervened through the confusion of languages. From this arose the various human cultural and ethnic groups as well as the languages known today. We are all one human race descended from Adam and Eve—through Noah and his family.

CHRIST - God came to earth—to the people of Abraham known as the Jews—to reach and save the lost. He also came to teach and show humans *"made in His own image"*[1] how they should behave. In Jesus Christ, God Himself became a human being.

CROSS - God, our Messiah, in the person of Jesus Christ, chose to die an excruciating, painful death as the penalty we deserve for our human sin. Once again—through Jesus—we can walk on a daily basis with God and be guaranteed eternal life. God loves each human whom He made in His image so much that He left the glory of heaven to become the *"last Adam."*[2] Jesus did not sin but took the penalty for sin that we all deserve. All of us, like Adam, have sinned and cannot pay for our own sins. We needed a perfect sacrifice to cover our sins. Jesus became that sacrifice.

CONSUMMATION - Jesus will come a second time to finish what God started and mankind ruined. Someday soon the prayer that Jesus taught us will come true, *"Thy kingdom come. Thy will be done in earth, as it is in heaven."*[3] God's will is certainly not being done on earth at the present. But there will come a day when planet Earth will be returned to the *"very good"*[4] state from which it started. There will be a *"New Jerusalem"*[5] and God's Kingdom—with Jesus Christ as its King of Kings—will last forever.

Amen - Come Lord Jesus

1. *Genesis 1:27*   2. *Romans 5:14-20, 1 Cor. 15:45*
3. *Matthew 6:10*   4. *Genesis 1:31*
5. *Revelation 3:12*

The First "C" - CREATION
(Genesis Chapters 1-2)

" Believing that a cosmic ray can
produce a favorable mutation is like
believing that it is sometimes a good
thing to drive nails through your
laptop."

- Alan Root

" There are fewer and fewer living
species with each passing year.
Working the numbers backwards,
until all the fossils are alive once
more, and you find yourself at
the beginning of Genesis."

- Alan Root

"In the beginning God created the heaven and the earth."[1] Only God could originate such a concept and only an infinite, omnipotent God could create the universe, in all of its ordered complexity, *"ex-nihilo"* (out of nothing). If we really respect the Word of God, Genesis should be read and believed exactly as it stands without trying to "interpret" it to fit some theory of men.

God started everything in the physical universe by exercising His creative power. By merely speaking he brought the universe into being. God focused His attention on planet Earth, carefully shaped it to support life and populated it with living creatures. Finally, God created humankind in His own image and set man to rule over His creation. The first chapters of Genesis emphasize the awesome power of our Creator, and yet reminds us that humans are the focus of God's loving concern.

God's revelation of Himself is the heart of Genesis 1. His majestic name is found there no less than 32 times, usually the subject of some active verb. He speaks, makes, separates, sets the sun and stars in the regularity of day following night, and season succeeding season. He displays His love and unselfishness by sharing His likeness with human beings. God affirmed our significance by sharing His own image with us. In everything we are reminded that God is a person, vastly intelligent, but also very caring and warm. The act of creation—like creation itself—reveals our God.

The Hebrew word used in Genesis 1:1 for God is "Elohim." This word is actually a plural noun, suggesting from the very first verses of the Bible that God is both a single entity and multifaceted in nature. The use of the plural Elohim strengthens our revelation that God is both energizing Spirit and omnipotent Creator. The tremendous events of creation week were, undoubtedly, first revealed by God to Adam in the Garden of Eden. His revelation to

Adam, as to Adam's origin, began with a description of the ex-nihilo creation of the universe on the first day and concluded with the creation of mankind on the sixth day. The man and woman were then placed in charge over all the earth, as stewards under God's ownership.

At least sixteen times Adam would have heard God relate the action which resulted from His speaking. God spoke to create, He spoke to identify, and He spoke to bless. Adam would have also recognized that the account was presented as an actual chronological history. The events of that wonderful week contained no hint whatsoever that God did not mean exactly what He said. Each section in the account begins with the Hebrew grammatical construction called the "waw" construction, which indicates a sequence of events. There is no suggestion of allegory, overlap, gap, or anything except straightforward history. Adam surely knew what a "day" was, but if there might be

THE EVOLUTION OF SCHOOL KIDS

any question, God defined the word for Him. *"And God called the light Day, and the darkness he called Night. And the evening and the morning were the first day."*[2] And thus God confirmed that these days were, and still are, literal days.

In order for Adam and Eve to *"have dominion over"*[3] the earth, they would have to learn what we now call "science". They would have to organize and utilize this knowledge in productive ways that would both benefit others and honor their Creator ("technology"), and they would have to disseminate this information and its products to others ("business", "education", "communication", "transportation," etc.). God said five times that different aspects of His work were "good" and then finally, after it was completed, He pronounced it all "very good." This divine evaluation was to be accepted by mankind and mimicked in works of music, art and literature. Our purpose is to glorify and praise God for all He has done. Since everything was "good," there was nothing evil; no disease, no competition, no lack of harmony, no deterioration, and above all, **NO DEATH** of living creatures.

At the end of chapter one, God rested from His creative work, not because He was tired, but so that He could set a pattern for the good of mankind. In chapter two, the author returns to look in greater depth at the creation of mankind. This chapter is not a second creation account, but a closer look at the most significant of God's works. Note how carefully God shaped Eden, to permit Adam to use those capacities of personage which the Lord created in Him. God endowed mankind alone with a love of beauty, delight in meaningful work, moral responsibility, and an incredible capacity for invention. Yet, despite these fulfilling gifts, Adam gradually realizes something was lacking, so

God made Eve, a "suitable helper" for him. God used the method of taking a rib from Adam in order to teach him that man and woman share a common identity; they are equals, each fully participating in God's image and likeness. Yet,

> *The intellect of Isaac Newton and Albert Einstein would have paled in comparison to Adam's intelligence.*

they are also different, so that a man and woman can bond together as husband and wife in order to meet each other's deepest needs for intimacy, lifelong commitment, and mutual support. Woman was designed to fully share in all that man is and vice versa. Each other's needs can be met only by lifelong commitment that God intended from marriage.

It seems likely that Adam knew how to write, for Genesis chapter two is called, *The Book of Adam,* and no one but Adam could have known about the events of this section. For him to be able to name animals and subdue the earth, as God commanded, he must have had extraordinary intelligence and skill. It has been said that Adam, before his fall, was the most brilliant human to have ever walked the face of the earth. The intellect of Isaac Newton and Albert Einstein would have paled in comparison to Adam's intelligence. Adam had come directly from the Creator's hand and was made directly "in His image." Surely he was capable of accurate, rapid, analytical reasoning, along with precise verbal and written communication. There is every reason to regard Genesis chapters 1 and 2 as being an accurate account of the events it describes. It is only evolution, with its assumption of our assent from brutish apelike creatures, which cause us to assume our forefathers were less intelligent than ourselves.

Adam and Eve were created as a full-grown man and woman (in my opinion without belly buttons). Animals also were made full-grown, immediately capable of *"multiplying upon the earth."*[4] To judge the sudden appearance of such a finished creation as impossible or unscientific is equivalent to saying God could not create in any manner He chooses. This is simply another form of atheism. The divinely inspired historical record clearly states that this was how it was done. That should be

AFTER EDEN
by Dan Lietha

www.AnswersInGenesis.org

In the beginning, the title of 'mother' was first given to one of these two choices. Do you know which one?

© 2001 AiG

Used by permission of AiG - www.AnswersInGenesis.org

Eve   Earth

Hint: The earth is not your mother.

And Adam called his wife's name Eve; because she was (to be) the mother of all living.
Genesis 3:20

sufficient for any believing Christian. However, there is abundant scientific evidence supporting the fact that every form of life was created recently and not millions of years ago. Both *Search for the Truth*[5] and *A Closer Look at the Evidence*[5] (see order information on page 148) provide fascinating documentation for those who wish to further examine this evidence in greater detail.

Adam and Eve were most certainly NOT formed by any evolutionary process from a population of hominids, as modern pseudo-intellectuals have deceived themselves into believing. However, before God formed Eve, He showed Adam the wide variety of the animals which He had formed earlier in the day. Adam was to exercise dominion over them, so God told him to give each a name appropriate to its individual characteristics. The animals brought to him included "all cattle... the fowl of the air, and...every beast of the field." Adam was in this way, introduced to all those animals that would live near him and might be possible candidates for companionship or usefulness. Not included were fish, wild beasts, or the creeping things (insects). Furthermore, only the created "kinds" were included, not the multitudes of genera, species, and varieties that later proliferated from the originally created kinds.

In view of the limited number of relevant kinds of cattle, field animals, and birds, and in view of Adam's giant intellect as well as divine guidance and instruction, the project of naming these creatures was quite within Adam's ability in a short period of time. An additional purpose of the assignments was to show Adam that he needed a suitable companion. After this, God proceeded to form Eve from Adam's rib and to give them to each other. **Out of one came two who are intended to live together as one.** Just as God provided a spouse for Adam, we should fervently seek God's guidance in our selection of our future husband or wife.

The basic human institution of marriage, making "one flesh" of husband and wife in lifelong union, is founded on the special creation of the first man and woman, for each other and for God. This then is the pattern, and norm, for all of the human descendants of Adam and Eve to follow. Marriage is of such great significance and sanctity that Jesus uses marriage as the model of His relationship between Himself (the groom) and the Church (His bride). Anything other than a single man and woman, married for life, is a perversion of God's intended design for our lives.

Once the literal creation of man and woman is denied, the factual historic basis for marriage is destroyed. At this point other possibilities, such as homosexual "marriages," become just another choice. If the account of the creation of man and woman is not an historical fact, then we have no factual basis upon which to form any marital arrangement. Anything from homosexual marriage to polygamy becomes a matter of opinion because there is no real event from which to judge what is right or wrong.

God told Adam and Eve to "be fruitful and multiply." There can be little doubt that they had a genuine love for each other in all its dimensions, and it would not have been long before Eve conceived a child. It was not to be the joyous occasion it could have been, however, for before the actual conception, the greatest tragedy of all history intervened.[6,7]

1. *Genesis 1:1*   2. *Genesis 1:5*   3. *Genesis 1:26*
4. *Genesis 1:28*
5. *SearchfortheTruth.net* shows several books documenting this evidence.
6. *The Bible Readers Companion*, Lawrence O. Richards, excerpts used from p.25.
7. *Biblical Creationism*, Henry M. Morris, excerpts and paraphrased from p.17-25.

The Second "C" - CORRUPTION
(Genesis Chapters 3-5)

" Evolution is accepted not because it
  can be proved by logical coherent
  evidence, but because the only
  alternative is incredible."

-D. M. S. Watson

" Evolution is unproven and unprovable.
  We believe it because the only
  alternative is special creation, and that
  is unthinkable."

- Sir Authur Keith

The innocence and harmony of the original creation were shattered when Adam and Eve chose to disobey God, resulting in consequences that still affect the entire human race. The Bible's account of the Fall of man is the correct explanation for sin and evils that mar every human society; corrupt personal and international relationships, and doom us to biological death and spiritual judgement. Genesis chapter 3 explores temptation, the impact of sin on relationships, the devastation of judgment, and the impact of human sin on nature itself. At the close of the chapter Adam and Eve are exiled from Eden. But first God Himself provides animal skins for clothing as a graphic demonstration that it is only by the shedding of innocent blood that sins can be covered.

Sin has many consequences, not the least of which is our alienation from God. **Only by fleeing to God, rather than from Him, can we find help.** Adam recorded his sad story in simple poignant words.

The temptation came through the serpent, the most "subtle" of the beasts of the field. It is unknown whether Adam and Eve had been informed about the invisible angelic realm, or the rebellion of their leader, Satan, who aspired to usurp God's reign. Being a powerful spirit being, Satan was able to speak in human language and Eve did not appear to be surprised. Perhaps this was her first direct contact with one of the creatures. To the young bride, the evil spirit in the serpent could communicate in such a clear way that she would assume it was the serpent speaking. Demonic communication has occurred with humans on various occasions throughout history. In any case, whatever the exact mechanism may have been, it was perceived as an actual conversation and he recorded it as such. The end result was both Adam and Eve eating the forbidden fruit from the tree of the knowledge of good and evil.

As a consequence of Adam and Eve doubting and disobeying God's commands, they died spiritually, in the sense that their fellowship with God was instantly broken. They also began to die physically as God withdrew His sustaining power and the law of decay started to work in their bodies. This process would ultimately take them back to the dust from which their bodies had been formed. But it was not just Adam and Eve who died. The effect of sin was transmitted to all their descendants, so that *"death passed upon all men."*[1]

The curse of sin affected everything in Adam's dominion. God said to Adam, *"cursed is the ground for thy sake."*[2] The serpent was *"cursed above every beast of the*

AFTER EDEN
by Dan Lietha

DO YOU JOHN, A SINFUL, FALLEN, IMPERFECT, SELFISH, DESCENDANT OF ADAM, TAKE THIS WOMAN, A SINFUL, FALLEN, IMPERFECT, SELFISH, DESCENDANT OF ADAM, TO BE YOUR LAWFULLY WEDDED WIFE...

www.AnswersInGenesis.org

© 2001 AiG

Used by permission of AiG - www.AnswersInGenesis.org

Reality weddings.

field"[2] indicating that all animals also came under the curse as a part of Adam's dominion. Their bodies, like that of Adam, had been made out of the *"dust of the ground."*[3] Thus the very elements, i.e. "the ground", were included in God's curse, thereby affecting everything in the physical universe. Because of Eve's key involvement, the process of reproduction was especially affected, so that what would have been a pleasant and painless experience become an experience of unique travail and suffering, not only for Eve, but, also, for all her descendants.

Because their intimate fellowship with God had been destroyed, Adam and Eve were banished from the beautiful paradise that had been planned as their home. Although the garden continued to exist, people were no longer allowed to go there, where they might partake of its life-sustaining *"tree of life."*[4] To do so would be to continue an eternal physical existence without God's fellowship.

In spite of their awful loss, Adam and Eve left the Garden with God's gracious promise of a coming Savior in their minds and hearts. This promise was faithfully recorded by Adam, even though he probably did not fully comprehend its meaning. The "serpent" who had participated in their Fall would himself eventually be crushed by one of their human descendants. Even more incomprehensible, this Savior would come from the *"seed of woman."*[5] In human terms, new life always came about from the "seed" (sperm) of man. This is the first promise of a coming Messiah was different because He must also be divine—the God/Man—God in human form. It is because the human sperm, carrying its curse of sin, was not involved in Jesus conception that he was born with a sinless nature.

God provided Adam and Eve with a covering for their nakedness. This clothing marked the very first time that physical death entered the world. Innocent animals (possibly even sheep) were put to death to cover the sins of

mankind. They shed their blood so that God could make skin "coats" for the guilty pair. This was the very first sacrifice, substituting the death of an innocent creature for the deserved death of a guilty sinner. Although Adam himself did not record anything more about specific sacrifices (that came later with Moses), God must have given him some explanation, because sacrifices to God have served as the pattern throughout all cultures and human history.

Not only did all of creation change for the worse, but in Genesis chapter four, the consequences of the Fall dramatically effected the descendants of Adam and Eve. Cain murdered his brother, Abel. Lamech broke the pattern of monogamous marriage by taking two wives. Humanity spiraled downward as Lamech justified his murder of a young man for injuring him.[6] The violent history of sinful human society throughout history is all too clear.

Adam and Eve must have longed for the coming of the promised redeemer, because they gave Seth a name of expectation (Seth means "appointed one"). In one sense, he was, since he became the person through whom the promise would eventually be fulfilled. At least some in his line would *"call on the name of the Lord."*[7] Centuries passed as God continued to preserve a family line which would ultimately lead to our Savior though a man of faith named Noah.

The Bible states that Adam and Eve *"begat (other) sons and daughters."*[8] Given the fact that there were far less diseases and genetic mistakes in the human body at that time, Adam and Eve lived for hundreds of years and most likely had dozens of children. Both Cain and Seth eventually married one of their sisters (or possibly, nieces) for there was no other way for Adam's children to fulfill God's command to multiply and fill the Earth. It was thousands of years later (at the time of Moses) that marriages between brothers and sisters became unlawful due to the harmful effect of the increasing number of mutations within their DNA.

Adam passed down to us, not the perfect image and likeness of God, but an image marred by his own imperfection. Today, we are still like God in many respects; but we are also like Adam, in desperate need of the Savior and His transforming touch.

The curse on nature also distorted our perception of work. God gave us work to be productive and satisfying. At its best, work reflects the joy God found in His creative work. At its worse the curse reduces work to drudgery: unending, unpleasant toil that brings neither fulfillment nor profit. At these times our experience of work should remind us of the burden of Adam's fall and our need for a Savior, Lord, and Redeemer.

Genesis chapter five consists of a lengthy genealogy in the narrative, which seems to have no great significance. However, every word of Scripture is of significance for those who understand the inspiration behind the text.

The entire Bible from cover-to-cover is about Jesus; the story of God's love and the redemption of mankind.

Chapter five is actually an astounding demonstration that the Bible is not just a collection of 66 books written by men; but it is a coordinated message from the Creator of the universe who is sovereign over the affairs of men. Chapter five contains the second of innumerable prophecies of our coming Messiah. Actually the entire Bible from cover to cover is about Jesus, the story of God's love and the redemption of mankind.

The Hebrew root of the names listed in Genesis chapter five each have ancient meanings. For instance many people know that Adam means ,**"man"** (because he was the first man) and Seth means, **"appointed"** (because Eve felt he was appointed to take the place of Abel). All of the other names in the genealogy leading to Noah similarly have Hebrew meanings:

> **Enosh** means *"mortal"* or *"miserable"*
> **Cainan** means *"sorrow"*
> **Mahalaleel** means *"the blessed God"*
> **Jared** means *"shall come down"*
> **Enoch** means *"teaching"*
> **Methuselah** means *"his death shall bring"*
> **Lamech** means *"despairing"*
> **Noah** means *"comfort (or rest)"*

Putting it all together we find that the very names of the first ten generations of mankind form an incredible message promising our coming Savior. **"Man (is) appointed mortal sorrow; (but) the blessed God shall come down, teaching (that) His death shall bring the despairing comfort."** [9]

The Genesis creation record is real history, not some esoteric allegory. It is an account of real people, real places, and real events at the very dawn of the history of God's created universe. This literal understanding of these primeval days is completely supported by both later references to them in God's revealed Word and by studying of the physical world around us. [10,11]

1. *Romans 5:12*   2. *Genesis 3:14,17*   3. *Genesis 2:7*
4. *Genesis 3:24*   5. *Genesis 1:15*   6. *Genesis 4:23*
7. *Genesis 4:26*   8. *Genesis 5:4*
9. *Hidden Treasures of the Bible*, Chuck Missler, p.10-30.
10. *The Bible Readers Companion*, Lawrence O. Richards, excerpts used from p.27-29.
11. *Biblical Creationism*, Henry M. Morris, excerpts and paraphrased from p.26-29.

The Third "C" - CATASTROPHE
(Genesis Chapters 6-9)

" The reason that most educated
    people believe in evolution is that
    they've been told that most educated
    people believe in evolution."

-Dr. Henry Morris

Genesis chapter six starts with a strange reference to "sons of God" taking "daughters of men" as wives. This obscure and extremely controversial passage is often interpreted as intermarriage between the *godly* line of Seth and the *sinful* line of Cain. Yet, many in the line of Seth were far from godly and every other reference to "sons of God" in the Old Testament refer to spiritual beings such as angels. Furthermore, Jewish commentators clearly understood this passage to mean that there was some kind of forbidden interaction between fallen angels and human women, which produced a race of Nephilim or Giants (fallen ones.) Noah was later referred to as "perfect in his generations", a reference more to his generational line than his moral obedience. Perhaps Satan desired to contaminate the human race to such an extent, that no savior could come through the seed of man. Apparently, Satan was involved in some sort of genetic manipulation of mankind because this same thing is also mentioned in Jude 1:6. Regardless of the exact meaning of this passage, God waited as long as possible before sending a flood to destroy the world. He planned to restart the human race through the only family which had both demonstrated faith through obedience and whose genetic line had not been compromised.[1]

The world before the Flood was described as wicked and violent. Sin always degenerates to this condition. The Hebrew word for wickedness is *rasah*, defined as criminal acts committed against others that violate their rights and profit from others' pain. The Hebrew word for violence is *hamas*, defined as willfully destructive acts intended to damage others. Any society marked by continual expressions of wickedness and violence is in peril of divine judgment.

The Bible places the creation of the universe at approximately 4000 B.C. The Genesis Flood is estimated to have taken place approximately 2300 B.C. Therefore it took mankind only 1700 years to become so corrupt that God finally warned them; *"My spirit shall not always strive with man, for that he also is flesh: yet his days shall be one hundred and twenty years."*[2]

It is when our faith is tested by years of working and waiting, that the quality of our faith is revealed.

This is the second specific reference in the Bible to the Holy Spirit. In the first, His Spirit was revealed as the one responsible for energizing and activating the created cosmos. Later God repeats his ominous warning: *"I will destroy man whom I have created from the face of the earth, both man and beast, and the creeping thing, and the fowls of the air; for it repenteth me that I have made them."*[3] God always gives a warning before bringing judgment because he is *"not willing that any should perish."*[4]

Before the great worldwide Flood (which is mentioned in every culture throughout the world) there were just ten generations who populated the planet in direct line to Jesus: Adam, Seth, Enosh, Cainan, Mahlaleel, Jared, Enoch, Methuselah, Lamech (the father of Noah) and Noah.

Adam lived 930 years, including his brief time in the Garden of Eden. A life span of this magnitude may seem too incredible to believe but scientists really do not know exactly what causes our bodies to wear out, so it is quite possible that people lived much longer when originally created. The world before the Flood was much more of a paradise and human genetic problems would not have had a chance to build up within our genes. Adam lived to know nine out of ten of the generations which preceeded the Flood. Noah was born in time to know every patriarch except Adam, Seth, and Enoch. Methuselah outlived his own son and did not die for 969 years, the very same year of the great global Flood. It would not have been at all surprising if the Flood started on the very day when Methuselah died. Enoch, Methuselah's father, was a prophet who apparently was given the first warning of the coming judgment because he named his son Methuselah, which literally means, *"His death shall bring (judgement)."* It is a testimony to God's mercy that the man whose death was prophesied to bring worldwide destruction would be the man who lived the longest of any human in history.

For over a hundred years before God sent the Flood, Noah undoubtedly preached of the coming judgement and need for repentance. Yet none listened. Noah is honored for his persistent faithfulness. He labored 120 years constructing a great ship on a waterless plain. He must have suffered merciless ridicule from his neighbors, none of whom responded to his warnings of the judgment to come. Yet his trust in God and obedience did not waver. Faith is always demonstrated by obedience. Without obedience, there is no faith. It's when our faith is tested by years of working and waiting, that the quality of our faith is revealed.

God instructed Noah, *"Make thee an ark of gopher wood; rooms shalt thou make in the ark...the length of the ark shall be 300 cubits [440 feet]; the breadth [width] of it 50 cubits [72 feet], and the height of it 30 cubits [44 feet]. A window shalt thou make to the ark, and in a cubit [1.5 feet] shalt thou finish it above; and the door of the ark shalt thou set in the side thereof; with lower, second, and third stories shalt thou make it."*[5] The ark was essentially a huge box (the Hebrew word

The ark was a HUGE vessel

itself implies it), designed for stability in the waters of the Flood rather than for movement through the waters. It was not the little cartoon boat so often featured in children's books.

The ark was taller than a normal four-story building and about 1 1/2 times as long as a football field. The total volumetric capacity was equal to 1,396,000 cubic feet, equal to that of 522 standard railroad stock cars. Since a standard stock car can carry 240 sheep, the ark could have carried over 125,000 sheep. The average size of all the animals on board the ark was certainly less than that of a sheep. It has been estimated that at the very most only 16,000 species of land animals (that is, birds, mammals, reptiles and amphibians) would have needed to go on board. It may have been much less.[6] The ark was certainly large enough to hold every type of created air breathing land animal. Remember that the ark would have not needed to contained every species or breed of animal, only prototype *"kinds"*[7]. Probably a single pair of cattle carried the genes that now provide for the wide variety and variation within this animal class such as Brahma, longhorn, Holstein, Jersey, etc. The biblical account of creation dispels the notion that all animal life evolved from single-celled ancestors. However, since the time of the Creation and the Flood, animals have varied widely within genetic limits set by God in order to allow them to survive in widely varying environments. For instance, wolves, dogs, coyotes, foxes, jackals, and dingoes probably all come from a single pair of dogs taken aboard the ark.

What about the dinosaurs? In the Bible they were known by Job as behemoths with tails *"like a cedar."*[8] The word dinosaur didn't come into existence until 1841, and simply means "terrible lizards."

There was no reason for Noah to have taken towering "grandfather sized" sauropods onboard the ark. Maturing juveniles would be small and fit easily into the space available in the ark. Dinosaurs hatch from eggs and even the largest sauropods egg was only the size of a football so even the largest dinosaurs were once small. Like many modern reptiles, dinosaurs probably kept growing until they died, so very large ones were simply very old. Large, old dinosaurs would not have been taken onto the ark. In fact, all dinosaur skeletons so far discovered indicate that the average size was that of a sheep, and almost all dinosaur fossils are found buried in flood deposits. Christians need not be afraid to share the biblical perspective on dinosaurs as a witness to the Bible's true account of this catastrophic event.

During the filming of a popular Hollywood film, "In Search of Noah's Ark," produced by Sun Classics, a scale model of the ark was built and placed into a large wave tank at Scripps Institute of Oceanography at LaJolla, Ca.

Giant waves, larger than anything experienced on a real ocean, were produced by a mechanical wave generating device. In spite of the size of these waves, the ark proved almost impossible to capsize. It was designed by God for stability rather than speed and its dimensions were ideal for that purpose.

The ark not only had space for two of every "kind" of air-breathing land animal but it also carried all of the necessary food for these animals. In addition, it provided living quarters for Noah and his family (eight people altogether). The Ark was large enough to carry many more people, but sadly no one accepted the invitation, and after the door closed it was too late.

After all the animals had settled in their "rooms," some probably began to sleep or hibernate. Most animals have been created with genetic potential for both migration and hibernation, if and when conditions warrant. The animals were directed by their Creator to migrate to the ark where many probably settled into a state of hibernation. After Noah and his family entered the ark, the Lord shut the door and the catastrophic Flood began.

"And the flood was forty days upon the earth; and the waters increased and bore up the ark, and it was lifted up above the earth...and the ark went upon the face of the waters...and all the high hills that were under the whole heaven were covered. Fifteen cubits (22 feet) upward did the waters prevail; and the mountains were covered. And all flesh died that moved upon the earth, both of fowl, and of cattle, and of beast, and of every creeping thing that creepeth upon the earth, and every man; all in whose nostrils was the breath of life, of all that was in the dry land, died. And every living substance was destroyed which was upon the face of the ground, both man, [and woman] and

cattle, and the creeping things, and the fowl of the heaven; and they were destroyed from the earth, and Noah only remained alive, and all that were within the ark. And the waters prevailed upon the earth for a hundred and fifty days." [9]

Can there be any doubt that the Bible is describing a devastating global flood and not just a local one? God made it clear that the Flood would cause "the end of all flesh," and that it would "destroy them with the earth." These statements made it clear that the Flood would be a worldwide Flood, not a local flood. The only plausible reason for constructing the huge vessel described in Genesis was to preserve all of the created kinds of animals for the

AFTER EDEN — by Dan Lietha

THE 'FLOOD' WILL NEVER HAPPEN! NOAH HAS BEEN WARNING US OF THIS 'JUDGEMENT FROM GOD' FOR DECADES NOW ...

© 2003 AiG

www.AnswersinGenesis.org

Used by permission of AiG - www.AnswersinGenesis.org

One message you never want to receive from God is, 'I told you so'!

future world. Such an ark would have been completely unnecessary if the flood were merely a regional event.

It is possible that, at the same time the Flood was covering the earth, a single land mass began to separate (today known as "plate tectonics"). This splitting gave rise to great bursts of water from the hitherto well regulated fountains from great subterranean reservoirs. These large land movements would have happened many orders of magnitude faster than anything we see happening on the earth today. Subterranean eruptions undoubtedly brought up other materials with the gushing waters, such as volcanic lava and volcanic dust. Dust particles blown into the sky may have served as condensation nuclei to trigger additional precipitation during the Flood. During the Flood the sea floor apparently also burst open at the mid-Atlantic and other ocean ridges, producing submarine lava as well as tsunami waves traversing the water surfaces. Those watching in the ark would only have been aware of a very small part of the tremendous geologic activities taking place around the globe.

The entire pre-Flood civilization (very conservatively estimated to be hundreds of millions of people) was destroyed. The ungodly men and women of that age surely tried desperately to escape the waters, fleeing to higher ground and riding on makeshift rafts or floating debris. Part of the reason the Flood lasted almost a full year was to ensure that no humans other than those upon the ark survived. Not many would be caught in the sediments because they would have moved to high ground as the Flood waters rose. Eventually all were drowned, but very few would have become fossilized. Their bodies would float on or near the surface until eaten by scavengers or severely decayed. The vast majority of fossils would have consisted of slow-moving lower ocean dwelling creatures, and that is exactly what we find. Over 95% of all fossils are bottom-dwelling sea creatures. At various times during the yearlong Flood, huge quantities of vegetation were buried to eventually form vast coal, oil, and gas fields. In addition to coal fields, there were enormous quantities of pre-Flood animal remains buried and fossilized under sediments. That is why we find billions of dead things buried in rock layers all over the earth. Even on the top of mountains we find fossilized sea life because these mountains were part of the ocean floor prior to and during Noah's Flood. All of the

The new Toutle River Canyon

world's mountain ranges were lifted up during and subsequent to the year long Flood of Noah.

Huge geological features, such as the Grand Canyon, did not form over millions of years by slow gradual erosion, but they formed rapidly as receding Flood waters tore through recently deposited sediments. The new Toutle River Canyon near Mt. St. Helens is an example of how rapidly river canyons can form. This 600-foot-deep canyon formed in one day as waters, that were backed up after the Mt. St. Helens explosion, broke through an earthen dam to carve a new river canyon through recently formed sediment layers. This canyon provides a small local model of the type of geological activities which were happening on a worldwide scale during the global flood.

After one hundred and fifty days, the waters started to abate and the ark came to rest upon the mountains of "Ararat." This area is the same as Armenia and it is possible that the ark is still trapped within the snow and ice on one of the mountain ranges of Armenia. Long after the Ark came to rest, additional earth movements continued around the globe restoring equilibrium to the distorted and displaced crust of the earth. New continental structures and mountains rose, accompanied by the opening of new ocean basins into which the floodwaters drained. All of the heat released from this tectonic activity would have heated our oceans—causing increased evaporation—which in turn, would have provided ideal conditions to trigger an ice age lasting for hundreds of years after the Flood. this single Earth ice age lasted until the volcanic activity subsided and the oceans cooled.

Noah and his family had spent over a year in the ark waiting, first, for the rain to stop, then for the waters to recede, and finally for the ground to dry sufficiently for them to leave. Once a returning dove had found plant life, presumably from seeds or cuttings carried by the waters and deposited on the earth's surface, Noah then knew the animals could also find food to eat as they scattered out from Ararat. A new and devastated world laid before them as they opened the door of the ark. The ark was left high on Mt. Ararat, very near the geographic center of the earth's new land areas. It is possible that the remains of this ark still exist as a witness to future generations of the consequence of sin.

The new world was drastically different from the *"very good"* world they had known before. Barren and cold, rugged and forbidding, it seemed only a devastated remnant of what it once had been. But the wickedness of its inhabitants had been vanquished and God had preserved Noah though the destruction.

> *It is only by acknowledging that there has been a worldwide Flood that we can correctly interpret geology, anthropology, paleontology and the age of the earth.*

One of Noah's first activities was to build an altar and offer a *"burnt offering"* to the Lord. This faith offering was *"a pleasing aroma"* to God, and God made a *"rainbow"* covenant with Noah to never again destroy the earth with water.[10] Today, the rainbow still reminds us of God's commitment to never again destroy all life on Earth by a worldwide flood. There have been thousands of local floods since the great one of Noah. If the Flood described in Genesis was just a "local event" then our God is a liar.

Many years passed before the incident when Noah became drunk and passed out naked. Ham took pleasure at his father's fall from the pedestal of righteousness. Shem and Japheth acted in a more appropriate manner and gently covered their father with a garment without even looking at him. Ham's carnal delight at his father's drunkenness evidenced a fatal weakness in his own character: lack of respect for his father, and rebellion toward his father's God. Noah had probably already detected a similar attitude in Ham's son Canaan. The sins of a parent are frequently amplified in their children. Accordingly, God led Noah to pronounce a blessing on Shem and Japheth, but a curse on Ham (through his son Canaan). Noah felt it appropriate to note that just as Ham had grieved his father, so Ham would be grieved by his son.

A study of the nations which descended from each son reveals that Ham's descendants are primarily characterized by their physical contributions to the world; Japheth's descendants by their intellectual achievements, and Shem's descendants by their spiritual interests. This is essentially what was prophesied by Noah. Shem and Japheth would be servants to God. Ham would be a servant providing the physical substructure (agriculture, navigation, construction, business, etc.) upon which the intellectual and religious superstructure of the world could be erected. The word "servant" in these verses, incidentally, does not mean "slave" in the Hebrew, but "steward."

Noah died 350 years after the Flood at the age of 950. Only Jared and Methuselah lived longer. The Bible documents a drastic reduction of longevity for all post-flood mankind. Some have suggested this may have been due to the drastically changed world environment but it is more likely be the result of increasing genetic mistakes. Originally, both men and animals were told to eat only plants, but after the Flood eating meat was allowed. It is even possible that this change in human longevity was due to a shortage of available protein in the plants of the post-Flood world. This is a potentially fruitful area of research for creation scientists.

One very important addition was made by the Lord to the original Adamic mandate: *"Whosoever sheddeth man's blood, by man shall his blood be shed: for in the image of God he made man."* [11] Thus, capital punishment was not only authorized, but commanded by God for the crime of murder. The death penalty does not cheapen life but places such a high value on human life so as to make the ultimate sacrifice the penalty for taking the life of another. This command implicitly established the institution of human government, replacing the patriarchal system which evidently had been ordained for the pre-Flood civilizations, but which had deteriorated into anarchy. The biblical mandate is for government to be God's instrument on Earth to maintain order and provide justice.

Any other supposed purpose for government is an unjustified expansion of the power which God meant for governments to have. God's people have always been given the responsibility to care for the poor, sick and abused. When governments take over this role (primarily because the church has failed in its responsibility) abuse is almost inevitable. However, the establishment of government, law, police, military, and various other forms of social services needed to maintain justice, restrain evil and protect the innocent (in addition to science, technology, business, education, and others already authorized) gave the human populations new types of honorable vocations.

Christians tread on dangerous ground when they allow "so-called science" to deny the plain and emphatic Bible teaching of the historical fact of a universal Flood in the days of Noah. Rejecting or neglecting this fact means rejection of not only the Genesis record, but also, the New Testament's testimony about that historical event.

It is only by acknowledging that there has been a worldwide Flood that we can correctly interpret geology, anthropology, paleontology and the age of the earth. The resources in the back provide abundant scientific evidence for the factual nature of this recent global flood. By denying that there has been a global Flood, we will come to the wrong conclusion in all of these areas of study. If we cannot trust the Bible when it clearly gives us a historical framework by which to understand the physical world, why should we trust anything else it has to say? [12,13,14]

1. *Learn the Bible in 24 Hours*, Chuck Missler, p.26-30.
2. *Genesis 6:3*
3. *Genesis 6:7*
4. *2 Peter 3:9*
5. *Genesis 6:14-16*
6. *Noah's Ark: A Feasibility Study*, John Woodmorappe
7. *Genesis 6:20*
8. *Job 40:17*
9. *Genesis 7:17-24*
10. *Genesis 8:20 - 9:17*
11. *Genesis 9:6*
12. *The Bible Reader's Companion*, Lawrence Richards, p.29.
13. *Biblical Creationism*, Henry M. Morris, excerpts and paraphrased from p.31-33.
14. *The Biblical Basis for Modern Science*, Henry M. Morris, excerpts and paraphrased from p.290-294.

The Fourth "C" - CONFUSION
(Genesis Chapters 10-11)

" I have lived, Sir, a long time, and the longer I live, the more convincing proofs I see of this truth—that God governs in the affairs of men. And if a sparrow can not fall to the ground without His notice, is it probable that an empire can rise without His aid?

We have been assured, Sir, in the Sacred Writings, that, 'except the Lord build the House, they labor in vain that build it.' I firmly believe this; and I also believe that without His concurring aid we shall succeed in this political building no better than the builders of Babel."

-Benjamin Franklin

The Flood was such a devastating cataclysm that the geography of the originally created earth no longer existed. The garden of Eden was gone. The original Tigris and Euphrates rivers were gone. The first regions called Assyria and Ethiopia (Cush) were gone. Thus, any claim that part of our present world is the actual location of the original garden of Eden does not take the global flood literally and should be rejected. The post-Flood world was barren and rugged, but when people found a region that looked somewhat like the world they remembered, they apparently gave the rivers the same names as the original rivers associated with the Garden of Eden.

In Genesis chapter 10, we are told of the fourth major interaction of God with His creation. This chapter finds mankind building a great tower in a city later known as Babel. The mud left over from the Flood had hardly dried from the greatest judgment of all time when humans were already headed into corruption again. What sinful beings we are.

It is widely accepted that shortly after the flood, a man named Nimrod headed a new rebellion against God's wishes. Nimrod was referred to as *"a mighty one in the earth,"*[1] and was either chosen as the king of all the "Shinarians" or acquired this position by force. As Ham's grandson, he (probably also his father, Cush) resented the curse pronounced by Noah on his family and resolved to lead a rebellion against God. He centered his kingdom at the city of Babel, refusing to follow God's command to: *"be ye fruitful, and multiply; bring forth abundantly in the earth, and multiply therein."*[2] Instead Nimrod said, *"Let us build a city and tower, whose top may reach unto heaven; and let us make us a name, lest we be scattered abroad upon the face of the whole earth."*[3]

In this declaration, Nimrod was not actually proposing to reach heaven with a tower; for he was not stupid. The words, *"may reach"* are not in the original Hebrew. What Nimrod probably had in mind was a tower unto the heavens —possibly a tower with a shrine at its summit dedicated to the heavens and to the worship of the host of heaven.

It is possible that this tower was Nimrod's way of establishing a the focal point for the cultural, political, and religious life in his kingdom. The entire human population at the time, only a century or so after the Flood, was concentrated in this one area. It is amazing to think of a one-world government and religious system that was involved in worshiping the creation (pantheism) rather than its Creator. No doubt Nimrod was subtle enough not to propose a blatant rebellion against God. Perhaps he suggested that honoring the beautiful starry heavens with the various stars and constellations, would be worshiping God. After all, God was invisible and far away, but they could see these signs and their symbolical representation emblazoned on the temple walls and ceiling. Is it possible that this is the origin of the signs of the Zodiac? Did people teach that these heavenly bodies were where the angelic host of heaven resided? When they observed the stars, did they believe they were seeing the gods who could influence and control their own lives on Earth?

If this is the path that lead mankind away from worship of the one true Creator, gods and goddesses soon followed which resided not only in the stars, but also, in other components of the creation: trees, rivers, animals, and so on. The actual presence of the demonic spirits following Satan in his rebellion against God could easily have converted these beliefs into various forms of animism, spiritism and idolatry. The downward spiral from truth eventually led to actual communication between evil spirits and humans who would yield to such influences.

Such a blasphemous project as this undertaking of King Nimrod could only have originated in the mind of Satan, himself, who has been at war with God ever since his first rebellion. He succeeded in causing Adam and Eve to fall into sin, and later almost succeeded in corrupting the whole world at the time of Noah. Now, once again, he was trying to get this new generation of men to rebel against God, using Nimrod as his willing tool.

Imagine the following as one possible thought process of Satan as he originally worshipped God at the very throne of heaven. Satan was created as *"the anointed cherubim that covereth"*[4] and was the greatest and most beautiful of all the angels whom God created. Evidently, Satan decided that he was as great as his Creator. In order for Him to delude himself into this false belief, he may have first convinced himself that God was not his Creator. If God was not his Creator, then he must have developed his beauty and strength by some process. Therefore, he would eventually develop into a being as great and powerful as the one on the throne (God). In other words, Satan may have reasoned that he evolved to his current position before deciding to challenge God. He has been using the same lie of evolution, in one form or another, to deceive humans into rejecting God's authority over our lives ever since his own fall from grace.

In Genesis chapter 11, God reveals his thoughts concerning the folly of mankind again attempting to become greater than their Creator: *"And the Lord said, behold, the people is one, and they have all one language; and this they begin to do; and now nothing will be restrained from them, which they have imagined to do... let us go down, and there confound their language, that they may not understand one another's speech."*[5]

If they could not communicate, they could not cooperate. Therefore, *"the Lord did there confound the language of all the earth: and from thence did the Lord scatter them abroad upon the face of all the earth."*[6]

Chapter 11 goes on to list 70 nations which were possibly 70 separate families in the population at Babel. The various family/nation units now had different languages—some suggest sixteen original languages, corresponding to one for each of Noah's sixteen grandsons. If Babel was indeed centered on Nimrod's apostate religious system, then the various family/nation groups would have carried that system with them into their new

AFTER EDEN
by Dan Lietha

The world's first language barrier problems actually came much earlier than the Tower of Babel.

lands to become the American Indians, Polyenesians, Incas, Africans, Orientals, etc. This could explain how a distorted astrological, pantheistic, spiritualistic evolutionary system originated and was carried into all the world.

There was surely at least one exception, however. Neither Noah nor Shem were participants in this new rebellion at Babel, so it is reasonable that their language did not change. This supports the conviction of the ancient Israelite scribes that Hebrew was the original language: a belief further supported by the fact that the names of the antediluvian patriarchs, as well as the later patriarchs leading to Abraham, all have specific meanings only in the Hebrew language.

Whatever the number of original languages and nations, that particular number could not be assumed to stay constant. Both nations and languages proliferated, but also deteriorated. This deterioration has affected every part of culture—human societies tend to head downhill physically, morally, spiritually, linguistically, and every other way— except at such times when new spiritual and moral energy is introduced into the world through the Holy Spirit.

Before we finish the fourth "C," let's look at how the human race began to inbreed in smaller groups because of the linguistic barriers. This inbreeding is what created the various ethnic and cultural groups we now find all over the world.

One distinct difference in people is their skin coloring, Many people think that people come in lots of different colors—red, yellow, black and white, etc. But all human beings have the same basic skin color—brown. It is caused by a pigment called melanin. All people except albinos have this pigment, just in different amounts. Assume that high levels of melanin are represented by capital letters and low levels by lower case letters. Each person receives a set of genes from their mother (A) and another from their father

(B). Thus, a person with the most possible pigment (very dark brown skin) would have AABB genes and the person with the lightest skin (very pale brown skin) would have aabb genes. The maximum variation would come from a person with AaBb marrying a person with AaBb. From the end of the flood to the Babel dispersion, the human race was one small interbreeding population and the genes were mixed among the population.

If we cannot defend the Bible in our scientifically advanced age, Christianity appears ignorant and irrelevant to the world around us.

After Babel, people dispersed according to people groups and intermarried because of language barriers. This also tended to concentrate genes of like characteristics—resulting in the loss of variety within each group. The darkest Nigerians would have had AABB skin genes so that all of their offspring also had this gene combination. With light skinned Scandinavians the combination became aabb. So starting with an original set of parents having a wide variety of gene combinations, every variation of skin shade could have been produced within a single generation. In the same way, plants and animals could have been created to multiply and fill the earth in all its ecologic and geographic variety.

Isn't it wonderful that God not only made us look different (to avoid monotony), but He also gave us the freedom of choice (to be with him or against him) so that we are not puppets. We have different eyes, ears, noses, mouths, etc. None of us looks alike with the exception of identical twins (the Lord has blessed our family with such a pair, my grandsons, Michael and Jacob Brockelsby). Even then they are distinct persons with distinctly different spirits and personalities (souls).

This brief overview covered the first eleven chapters of Genesis, and lays the creation foundation upon which the Gospel of Jesus Christ is built. Without this foundation we could not understand our need for a redeeming Savior tobring us back to our heavenly Father and His kingdom.

Most people in our churches don't understand that the Bible is a true history book. Christianity is not based upon myths or interesting stories. It is based upon real history. There was a real Adam to whom we are all related. There was a real garden and Fall which is why we are all sinners. There is a real curse, which is why there is death and suffering. There was a real global Flood and only those on the ark were saved from destruction. This Flood is the reason why the geology of our planet looks the way it does. There really was a confusion of the languages at the Tower of Babel and this is where all the various ethnic and cultural groups of human beings are derived. Yet we are one human race made in God's image.

Christians need to believe God's Word from Genesis through Revelation, and know how to defend it (especially Genesis one through chapter eleven). If we cannot do this in our scientifically advanced age, Christianity appears ignorant and irrelevant to the world around us. We are commanded by God to be trained to *logically* defend the Word of God (*1 Peter 3:15*). The Bible can indeed be trusted.

1. *Genesis 10:8*   2. *Genesis 9:7*   3. *Genesis 11:4*
4. *Ezekiel 28:14*   5. *Genesis 11:6-7*   6. *Genesis 11:9*

The fifth "C" - Christ

" The Bible is true. Upon that
sacred Volume I rest my hope of
eternal salvation through the
merits of our blessed Lord and
Saviour Jesus Christ. I bequeath
my body to the dust whence it
comes, and my soul to God who
gave it, hoping for a happy
immortality through the atoning
merits of our Lord Jesus Christ,
the Saviour of the World."

- Andrew Jackson

When Adam disobeyed God, the prefect fellowship he had enjoyed with his Creator was destroyed. God promised that one day someone would be born, a descendant of Adam, who would rescue His creation from the curse that God had placed on it (Genesis 3:15). This person is Jesus Christ—the Messiah.

God began to focus His plan of redemption on a specific group of people about 2000 B.C., when he called Abraham to form a nation set apart for God. It was through this nation that the Messiah would be born (Genesis 21:12), through Abraham and his son Isaac. From Isaac came Jacob, then Judah, Perez, Hezron, Ram, Amminadab, Nahshon, Salmon, Boaz, Obed, Jesse, and finally King David, approximately 1000 years after Abraham. God controls the timing for bringing about His plan of redemption and His plans will never be stopped.

God promised that David would always have a descendant on his throne (Jeremiah 23:5-6, 1 Chronicles 17:10-14.) The legal right to this throne passed through David's son, Solomon, and on to his descendants. Unfortunately, Jeconiah the great, great, grandson of Solomon, was so wicked that God punished him by declaring that none of his children would ever again sit on the throne (Jeremiah 22:17-30). This caused a "problem" since Joseph, the "legal father" of Jesus, was a descendant of Jeconiah. If Joseph had been Jesus' *biological* father, Jesus would have had the *legal* right to the throne, but would have been unable to occupy it due to being under Jeconiah's curse.

God solved this problem by choosing Mary. Mary was from the line of Nathan, another son of David whose linage God had not cursed. So Jesus has the legal right to sit on the eternal throne of David, through his adoptive father, Joseph, and the physically right to sit on the throne of

David, through his natural mother, Mary. In this way God's promise mentioned in both Jeremiah and Chronicles was fulfilled.

There are four special women which the apostle Matthew shows were in the direct lineage from Abraham to Christ (Tamar, Rahab, Ruth and Bathsheba). The first three were not Israelites, and all but Ruth led immoral lives before trusting the true God (and turning from their sins). The fact that God included them in the ancestry of His Son, shows that God places equal value on both men and women, *unlike* almost every other culture and religion in the world. God's ability and desire to forgive sinners is also apparent.

Throughout the Old Testament there are prophecies of the coming Messiah. What better way for God to authenticate the Bible than to write down history in advance? This shows that God is outside of time and knows exactly what each of us are going to experience in advance. Several hundred very specific prophecies concerning the promised Messiah were made between 400 and 4000 years before Jesus was born. Every single one of these prophecies came true exactly as foretold. A few of

INSPECTING THE OFFENSIVE EVIDENCE

those prophecies are listed on the next page along with the Scripture verses showing how they came true. God foretold that the Messiah would be:

Prophecy	Made	Fulfilled
Born in Bethlehem	Micah 5:2	Matthew 2:1.
Presented with gifts	Psalm 72:10	Matthew 2:1,11
Called "Lord" - a reference to his deity	Psalm 110:1	Luke 2:11.
Called "Almighty God" or "Father of Eternity"	Isaiah 9:6	John 20:28
Born of a virgin and called "Emmanuel"	Isaiah 7:14	Matthew 1:23
Ride into Jerusalem on the foal of a donkey	Zech. 9:9	Matthew 21:15
Pierced in His hands and feet	Psalm 22:16	compare to the crucifixion
Killed 483 years (69x7) after the order to rebuild Jerusalem	Dan. 9:24-27	Historical records show this was fulfilled
Thrust through or pierced	Zech. 12:10	John 19:34
Called "a prophet like Moses" (i.e. who would receive face-to-face revelation from God the Father)	Deut. 18:18	Matthew 21:11, Acts 3:22, John 8:28, John 12:49
Called priest	Psalm 110:4	Hebrews 3:1.
Preceded by messenger (John the Baptist)	Isaiah 40:3	Matthew 3:1-2

Our only glimpse of the childhood of Jesus comes from Luke chapter 2:41-52, where we first hear of our Lord when He is approximately twelve years of age. He and His parents go to the Passover festival, and while returning, His parents find Him missing from the traveling party. They returned to Jerusalem and find Him three days later in the

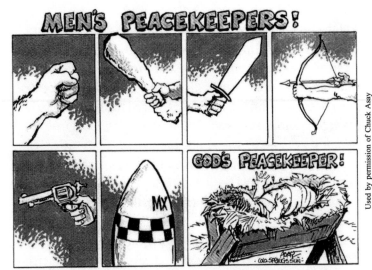

temple among the teachers, listening and asking questions.
All who heard Him were amazed at His understanding and
His answers. His mother Mary was upset and said, *"Son,
why hast thou thus dealt with us? behold, thy father
and I have sought thee sorrowing."* He said to them,
*"How is it that ye sought me? Did ye not know that I
must be about my Father's business?"*[1] They did not
understand what he was telling them. Afterwards, Jesus
obediently returned to Nazareth and His mother treasured
all these things in her heart. *"And Jesus increased in
wisdom and stature, and in favour with God and man."*[1]

Let's turn to the gospel of John for the description of the
remainder of our Lord's ministry. This Gospel was written
thirty years after the accounts of Jesus written by Matthew,
Mark, and Luke. More than any other, this Gospel speaks
directly to the disbelief so prevalent in our society today.

The Gospel of John begins in the same place as Genesis
chapter one verse one. *In the beginning* there was only
God and *everything* was made by Him. After confirming
this fact, the narrative goes immediately to John the Baptist
who testified to the identity of the one who made the world.

Yet the people who should have known the Creator best, the Jews, knew Him not. The Word *(Jesus)* was made flesh and dwelt among us. *But to those who receive him, that believe on his name, he gives them power to be the sons of God.* John the Baptist prepared the way and first revealed who Jesus was: *"Behold the Lamb of God, which taketh away the sin of the world."*[2]

Jesus started his ministry by calling disciples to follow Him. He performed His first miracle at the wedding in Cana. Jesus' mother was somewhat rebuked by Jesus for her request for more wine for the guests, and she is never shown again requesting or demanding anything from Jesus. The only recorded command from Jesus' earthly mother, is this one: *"Do whatever Jesus says!"*[3]

This was the first of seven great "miracles," or "signs" recorded in John. The other six are in John 4:49-54; 5:5-9; 6:5-14; 6:16-21; 9:1-7; 11:41-44. This first miracle was a miracle of creation (as distinct from miracles of providence, which only control rates and timing of natural processes). It required direct creative power to supersede natural laws, perhaps by causing an instantaneous increase of complexity by changing the simple molecular structure of water into the very different elements of wine.

Later Jesus drove the traders from the temple—which he called His *"Father's House."*[4] Nicodemus visited Jesus by night and Jesus explained to him (as well as us) that, *"Except a man be born again, he cannot see the Kingdom of God...Except a man be born of water and of the Spirit, he cannot enter the Kingdom of God. That which is born of flesh is flesh; and that which is born of the Spirit is spirit."*[5]

John the Baptist, who baptized Jesus, further proclaimed who Jesus was and stated that the Lord's ministry must increase while his must decrease. In the same way the

desires and priorities of believers need to give way to the greater will of God for our lives.

Chapter four tells us about Jesus' encounter with the woman at Jacob's well. From this encounter we learn that Jesus is the *"living water,"*[6] and that he is the only one who can satisfy our thirst for fellowship with God.

Chapter five covers Jesus healing a lame man at the pool in Bethesda on the Sabbath. This is when Jesus made His relationship with His Father known to the Jews who then sought to kill Him because He claimed to be God (John 5:18). Jesus told them they did not understand the Scriptures for had they understood Moses' writings, they would have believed Jesus' words, because Moses wrote about Jesus.

Chapter six covers Jesus feeding the multitude, walking on the water, and telling the people that He was the bread of life. Many followers were unwilling to believe who He claimed to be and started to drift away.

In chapter seven, even Jesus' own brothers refused to believe that He is God. As Jesus preached in the temple the Jewish leaders questioned Jesus and tried to arrest Him. This is when Jesus told them, *"If any man thirst, let him come unto me and drink. He that believeth on me, as the scripture hath said, out of his belly shall flow rivers of living water."*[7] This is also when Nicodemus came to defend Jesus.

Chapter eight covers the forgiveness of the woman caught in adultery. Jesus frankly states, *"I am the light of the world,"*[8] and He told the Jews not to be slaves of sin. They claimed that Abraham was their father, but Jesus rebuked them by saying, *"before Abraham was, I am."*[9] The Jews immediately understood the implication that Jesus was again claiming to be the Creator God, and they again tried to stone him to death.

In chapter nine Jesus healed the man born blind, and the Pharisees questioned the blind man's family. Jesus explained that there is greater blindness than physical blindness in this world. Like the Pharisees who asked our

Lord, *"Are we blind also?"*[10] We must ask Him the same question of ourselves.

Chapter ten records the parable of the Good Shepherd. Again, the Jewish leaders tried to stone Jesus because He made yet another claim as to His deity.

In chapter eleven we are confronted with the death of Lazarus. Martha and Mary were very upset over the death of their brother because Jesus had not come in time to heal

> *Jesus was not hated for what he did but for who he was - the Creator God who was and still is the ultimate authority over mankind.*

him. At this point, we must take heed of what Jesus told Martha: *"I am the resurrection, and the life: He that believeth in me, though he were dead, yet shall he live: and whosoever liveth and believeth in me shall never die. Believest thou this?"*[11] Jesus modeled complete faith in God the Father. He then commanded Lazarus to, *"Come forth."*[12] When Lazarus arose and the Pharisees heard about this miracle, instead of praising God, they began in earnest to plot Jesus' death.

Chapter twelve covers Mary's anointing of Jesus' feet. This is the point in the narrative at which Jesus made his triumphant entry into Jerusalem on the foal of a donkey. This happened on the exact day prophesied by an angel almost 500 years earlier in Daniel 9:25-26.

At this point, Jesus predicted His death and subsequent resurrection. Some people believed while most others did not. On which side of this issue do you stand? Jesus still offers us eternal life in paradise, but we must choose to accept His offer.

In chapter thirteen Jesus washed the disciples' feet. Instead of serving each other, the disciples had been arguing who would be the greatest among them (Luke 22:24-27). The action of their master convicted them and they never again argued over this issue.

Next we go to the last supper. We still celebrate communion in honor and memory of what Jesus did and continues to do for us. Things proceeded rapidly to a conclusion from this point. We find that there was a deceiver among the disciples and that Peter would deny Jesus that very night.

Chapter fourteen clearly tells us that *Jesus is* *"the way, the truth and the life."*[13] He also tells us that the comforter (Holy Spirit) will come into our lives if we choose to believe in Jesus. We receive this Holy Spirit when we are truly born again (or literally "born from above"). This chapter ends with Jesus leaving His peace with us, just as many Christian church services end each Sunday with that same promise.

In chapter fifteen we learn that Jesus is the vine and we are the branches. We cannot survive without Him. The chapter ends with the Lord's command to love one another. This Christian love is too seldom portrayed today. Today "love" is portrayed as sex. See 1Corinthians, chapter 13, for a true definition of love. True love puts the needs of others above their own. True love has nothing to do with sex or self gratification. Jesus' entire life was a demonstration of true love.

Chapter sixteen completed Jesus' earthly ministry. He told His disciples about His leaving and returning, which they did not understand, but later their sorrow would be turned to joy. He also told them that, *"In the world ye **shall have tribulation** but always be of good cheer; I have overcome the world."[14]* It is a naive and shallow faith which expects problem free prosperity and acceptance by the world once making Jesus the Lord of their life.

Chapter seventeen in the Gospel of John is the *"Prayer Chapter."* This is the real Lord's prayer where He prays to the Heavenly Father, not only for Himself and His disciples, but also for us, His future followers. This chapter closes with, *"And I have declared unto them [His followers] thy name, and will [continue to] declare it: that the love wherewith thou has loved me may be in them, and I in them."[15]*

1. *Luke 2:41-52* 2. *John 1:29* 3. *John 2:5*
4. *John 2:13-16* 5. *John 3:3-6* 6. *John 4:14*
7. *John 7:37-38* 8. *John 8:12* 9. *John 8:58*
10. *John 9:40* 11. *John 11:25-26* 12. *John 11:43*
13. *John 14:6* 14. *John 16:33* 15. *John 17:26*

The Sixth "C" - The Cross

" Unto him that loved us, and washed
us from our sins in his blood, and
hath made us kings and priests unto
God and his Father; to him be the
glory and dominion forever and ever.
Amen."

- Revelation 1:5-6

The Gospel of John now comes to the primary reason Jesus came to earth. Jesus moved toward the fulfillment of the plan of redemption which God determined before time began. Knowing what He was about to face, Jesus pleaded with His Father not to have the sins of the entire world placed upon Himself. Were there any other way for God to reconcile Himself to us this plea would have been answered and Jesus would not had to have died His horrible death. In John, chapter eighteen, Jesus is arrested, Peter cut off Malchus' right ear, and Jesus immediately healed the ear and rebuked Peter, saying, *"Put up thy sword into the sheath: the cup which my father hath given me, shall I not drink it?"[1]*

Next, Jesus is put on illegal trial by Annas who was the father-in-law to Caiaphas, the high priest. Caiaphas inadvertently gave prophetic utterance to the Jews by saying that, *"it was expedient that one man should die for the people."[2]* Meanwhile Peter is busy denying his Lord, as predicted. Jesus is next sent before Pilate who tried to find a politically correct way to free Jesus.

In chapter nineteen we learn that Jesus is beaten and mocked. This is where the Jews demanded that Pilate crucify Jesus. Pilate had a difficult time condemning Jesus (because he was innocent) and he asked the Jews: *" 'Shall I crucify your King?' The chief priest answered, 'We have no king but Caesar.' "[3]* Backed into a corner, Pilate delivered Jesus to be crucified.

Jesus carried His cross as far as He could toward the place of the skull, which was called Golgotha in Hebrew. Jesus was nailed between two thieves with a title placed over His head on the cross. Pilate had written in Hebrew, Greek and Latin that this was: *"Jesus of Nazareth the King of the Jews."[4]* The chief priests wanted Pilate to change the wording to state that, "Jesus said He was the King of the Jews," but Pilate refused to change it.

At this point in the narrative, the Gospel of Luke illustrates the faith and forgiveness that our Lord provided. One of the thieves on the cross mocked Jesus saying, *"If thou be Christ, save thyself and us. But the other answered and rebuked him, saying, Dost not thou fear God seeing thou art in the same condemnation? And we indeed justly; for we receive the due reward of our deeds: but this man hath done nothing amiss. And he said unto Jesus, Lord, remember me when thou comest into thy Kingdom. And Jesus said unto him, Verily I say unto thee, Today shalt thou be with me in paradise."*[5]

All that our Lord asks from us is to trust and believe in Him and He will do the rest. Real trust and belief always results in a changed life. If there is no repentant action following a profession of faith, it is unlikely that any real change of heart or salvation has occurred. Even the thief on the cross acted by professing his faith in the face of ridicule.

This man demonstrated a changed heart. It was not his action that saved him, but the fact that real faith was demonstrated by his action. True faith and salvation always lead to action. As the Bible clearly states, *"Faith without works is dead,"[6]* and, *"Without faith, no one can please God."[7]*

Jesus being nailed to the cross looked down upon His mother and John, and said, *"Woman, behold thy son!"[8]* Then turning to look at John He said, *"Behold thy mother!"[9]* and from that hour John took her into his own home. Right up until the very last moment of His excruciating death, Jesus was thinking not of Himself but of others. This is the model Jesus gave us, we are to die to self daily and live for Him. Once we learn to live in this way, anything we ask of Him, He will give to us, because what we ask will be in line with the Lord's will for our lives.

Now with all things accomplished, Jesus said, *"I thirst."[10]* Upon receiving a mixture of vinegar-water He said, *"It is finished"[11]* (this final word uttered by Jesus was also commonly used on a bill of sale to mean, *"paid in full"*). After this statement, Jesus died.

Seeing that Jesus was dead, His legs were not broken as was the custom at crucifixions (commonly done so that victims would die quickly). This fulfilled the Jewish Passover requirement that the sacrificial lamb would have no bone broken (Exodus 12:46, Numbers 9:12, Psalm 34:20 and John 19:36). Jesus is our Passover sacrifice. It is His substitutionary death which allows God's righteous judgement to "pass over" us, but only if we accept Jesus as our Savior. The soldiers pierced His side with a spear, and a mixture of blood and water spilled out. Thus, the Scriptures, written hundreds of years before Jesus was even born, were precisely fulfilled when they spoke of *"A bone of him shall not be broken"[12]* and *"They shall look on Him whom they pierced."[13]*

It is said by some medical authorities that in the case of heart rupture, and in that case only, the blood collects in the pericardium, the lining around the wall of the heart, and divides into a sort of bloody clot and a watery serum. If this in fact happened, then the actual physical cause of Jesus' death was a ruptured heart. Under intense pain and extreme stress, his heart burst open. It may be that Jesus, literally, died of a heart broken over the sins of the world. Suffering for the combined sins of every human and the total separation from God, is more than the human body can stand.

Jesus came to earth to pay a debt we could not pay. His last spoken word on the cross was "tetelestia" which literally means "Paid in Full"

In the crucifixion there may even be a mystic parallel to Genesis 2:21-22. As God took from Adam's side, in his sleep, that from which He made a bride for Adam, so He took from Jesus, in sleep on the cross, that from which He made the bride of Christ—the church.

In chapter twenty we go from the cross to the resurrection where Mary Magdalene was the first to talk with the resurrected Christ. Later the disciples, including doubting Thomas, became totally convinced that Jesus has indeed risen from the dead. Jesus displayed a glorified body that could move solid walls and instantly appear anywhere. Chapter twenty-one covers the appearance of Jesus early in the morning to the disciples at the Sea of Tiberias. He commanded Simon Peter three times to feed His sheep. It is no coincidence that Jesus asks Peter, "Do you love me?" the same number of times for which Peter denied the Lord. At this time the Holy Spirit had not come upon the disciples but they would soon receive the power they needed to witness to the entire world. They truly become *"fishers of men,"* [14] each later dying for their faith.

It is the Holy Spirit that gives Christians confidence to live life in a selfless way—serving God rather than themselves. It is the literal resurrection of Jesus Christ which gives Christians the confidence to face death without fear. The assurance of our forgiveness, paid for by Jesus on the cross, and the reality of life after death, demonstrated by the resurrection of Jesus, give us that confidence. Such confidence results in hope, rather than despair at the death of loved ones. Such confidence was displayed by my niece, Nichole Asgaard, who wrote this poem about her grand mother Liana's unexpected journey to heaven:

God sure does have an 'angel',
You meant the world to us,
So when God took you home with Him
Why shouldn't we cause a fuss?

You were always there to listen
Talk, laugh and care,
But right now we are just hurting,
And it doesn't seem too fair.

We know it's what you wanted
And we know you are at peace,
We know you're there with Grandpa
Having such a feast.

It's hard to believe that all these years
Have gone and passed us by,
But every time we think of you
We all look up towards the sky.

So Gram keep a watchful eye
On all of us left here,
And we will keep your memories
Close and very, very near.

We know you are in heaven
Singing your happy tunes
And before we even know it,
We'll be there to see you soon.

1. *John 18:11*
2. *John 18:14*
3. *John 19:15*
4. *John 19:19*
5. *Luke 23:39-43*
6. *James 2:2b*
7. *Hebrew 11:6*
8. *John 19:26*
9. *John 19:27*
10. *John 19:28*
11. *John 19:30*
12. *Psalm 34:20*
13. *John 20:37*
14. *Matt 4:19*

The Seventh "C" - The Consummation

" It is impossible to rightly govern the
world without God and the Bible."

- George Washington

" There is but one straight course, and
that is to seek truth and pursue it
steadily."

- George Washington

" It is impossible to account for the
creation of the universe, without the
agency of a Supreme Being. It is
impossible to govern the universe
without the aid of a Supreme Being.
It is impossible to reason without
arriving at a Supreme Being."

- George Washington

In order to understand the consummation of all things (as described in Revelation) it would be helpful to first read the book of *The Acts of the Apostles*. Under the guidance of the Holy Spirit, Luke documented what Jesus did and taught when he was on planet Earth in the *Gospel of Luke*. He then wrote the book of Acts to summarize the growth of the Christian church in the first century. The book of Acts records numerous miracles, making this book hard to accept for people who reject the idea of God's supernatural intervention in history. However, because the critical importance of this time in history, the beginning of "His Bride," the church, it is to be expected that God would confirm the church through unique signs. When Jesus returned to heaven He sent the Holy Spirit to indwell, guide and empower His disciples (and us) to effectively preach the saving gospel message.

Two thousand years later we are still in this church age and God still works through His believers to perform miracles. At some point in the future His believers will be removed from this world, and the last step in the process of restoration (the consummation of all things) will begin. The book of Revelation, recorded by John, covers the restoration of all things to God's perfection and the consummation (fulfillment) of all His purposes in creation. This book explains what is going to happen at the end of the church age when the influence of true believers is removed from this world.

Revelation is prophetic in nature and, as a result, its interpretation is controversial. Unfortunately, many churches simply ignore it. It is a grave mistake to ignore Revelation, for prophecy becomes more and more important as the time of prophetic fulfillment nears. Although we do not know exactly when our Lord will return, every indication is that the time is rapidly approaching. Prophecy is nothing to be afraid of, it is simply God's way of confirming that the Bible is truly His revelation to us by writing down history in advance.

This last book of the Bible gets its name from the Greek word "apokalypsis" which means an "unveiling" of something previously concealed. It can also be translated as "the coming of our Lord Jesus Christ." Revelation is not about things Christ already told us but the revealing, unveiling, and/or appearing of Christ for the second time in human history.

Jesus came to planet Earth to rescue God's children from the opposing kingdom of Satan. With Christ's first coming, the kingdom of God has already dawned. Satan, the great usurper of God's authority, has already been defeated. The actualization will take place in two stages, a preliminary one which is still taking place, starting with Jesus' death and resurrection, and the completion of the kingdom which must still take place. Our Heavenly Father will bring everything to completion at a time of His

Used by permission of Chuck Asay

choosing. In the meantime, Jesus' followers (true Christians), must battle against Satan by the spiritual authority which Jesus has already given to us. When God the Father establishes His Kingdom here on Earth, this Kingdom will be given to His Son to rule.

People today are interested in the future and also quite afraid of it. Where is the world headed? How will it all end? Will Russia take over the Persian Gulf? Will the Arab nations continue to raise oil prices until everyone goes bankrupt? What about the increasing number of earthquakes and other natural disasters, and the skyrocketing rate of moral decay all around us?

God does not want us to be fearful about the future. Approximately one-quarter of the Bible is prophecy. Bible prophets have been 100% accurate in their predictions in the past, so we can be assured that the Bible will be 100% accurate about future predictions. The Bible prophets have been, and continue to be, vindicated in today's newspapers.

It was long ago prophesied that Israel would never disappear as a nation. After almost 2000 years in exile, they became a nation again in 1948 and regained control of Jerusalem in 1967. This is nothing short of a miracle. Many Bible scholars believe that our Lord's second coming will take place while the generation that saw the return to Israel is still living. This would be at most 100 years from 1948 (by 2048), but it could happen at any time.

Nobody knows, except the Heavenly Father, the timing of this future Kingdom. All we can do is look for the telltale signs which are written in Bible prophecy. When this Kingdom comes, God will destroy this fallen world, spoiled by Satan and his followers, and create a new one similar to the world before the Fall. In some wonderful way we are to participate in this transformation .

The final stage of human history will be a period of great trial and tribulation as God wakens and draws His last believers unto Himself. A horrendous release of evil will take place as soon as the restraining power of the Holy Spirit is removed. After this devastating seven-year tribulation period, the land of Israel will arise in a new and glorious splendor, and Jerusalem will be the center of this new kingdom. Everyone will come to acknowledge Jesus Christ as Lord. No sadness or sin will prevail, and all those left in this kingdom will behold the living God and serve Him in eternal righteousness, innocence, and bliss. Our hope is to be gathered with the church of Jesus Christ into this Heavenly Kingdom. We can join the early Christians in saying, *"THY KINGDOM COME!"*

In Revelation 1:3 it is written, *"Blessed is he that readeth, and they that hear the words of this prophecy, and keep those things which are written therein, for the time is at hand."* Shown below is a schematic of the true history of the universe:[1]

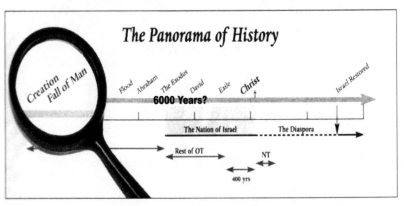

We are now in the church age (The Diaspora). When the rapture takes place all those believing in the Messiah, Jesus Christ, will be taken up in the twinkling of an eye. This will give the evil one (called the "Anti-Christ") full reign on planet Earth for seven years. Most biblical scholars admit that the straightforward understanding of Scripture describes a second return of Jesus after the seven year tribulation period to rule the earth from Jerusalem for 1000 years. After that period of time (called the Millennium) there will be the Great White Throne Judgment at which time everyone, living and dead, will be called into account for their actions.

If the blood of Christ does not cover the sins of a person's life, they will be held accountable at this Judgment Day. Those covered by the blood of the Spotless Lamb (Jesus Christ) will spend eternity with Christ in His new creation. Those who have not given their lives to Christ, and have not been covered by His blood sacrifice, will spend eternity in separation from their Creator (in hell). There will be an eternal home in the new heaven and new earth for all believers, which will be a realm of perfect joy because we will be doing what our Creator made us to do under His perfect leadership. Will you be part of this glorious future?

AMEN!!! *Come, Lord Jesus*

1. *Learn the Bible in 24 Hours,* Chuck Missler, p.1.

Chapter 4:
Christ is the Center

Long ago in Bethlehem born in low degree,
God in man came to earth to set us captives free.

Inspired of God, the prophet foretold how Messiah would come one day:
as it is written, it came to pass—no matter what men might say.

Our Savior foretold in Prophecy, to the things that are to be;
and now is coming to pass—for all the world to see.

He said nation would rise against nation, and iniquity would abound;
that there would be famine and earthquakes, and false prophets with doctrines unsound.

As it was in the days of Noah when man thought himself all-wise,
He will come like a thief in the night, and His bride, the church, shall rise.

Then tribulation will curse all the earth like no man has ever known.
For with great travail and anguished cries, even loved ones will betray their own.

But such shall hail the King of Kings, who was born in low degree.
Every knee shall bow, each tongue confess that Jesus Christ is He.

God is not man that He should lie, so do not be deceived.
You too, will confess that Jesus is Lord—even if you haven't believed.

For He shall appear to all mankind from the greatest unto the least.
As lightning shining unto the west that cometh out of the east.

So watch the eastern sky O race of modern men,
*as it is written, it shall come to pass—**Jesus Is Coming Again!**"*

Myra Eaves Bumgardner

The entire Bible is the account of one man. It has been said that every page points to Jesus Christ, either directly, prophetically, or symbolically. The Old Testament is Christ *concealed*—a true account of the beginning of everything, including the forming of the nation through which He was to come. The nation of Israel was founded and nurtured by God to bring *that man* into the world. The New Testament is Christ *revealed*—an account of what was accomplished through *that one man*.

One of the benefits of God becoming a man was to give us a concrete, definite, tangible model of what kind of a person to think of, when we think of God. God the Father is like Jesus. The Holy Spirit is the essence of Jesus. Jesus is God in human form. His appearance on earth was the central event of all history. The Old Testament sets the stage for it. The New Testament describes it.

We can either joyfully acknowledge Jesus as Lord of our lives now, or, in sorrow, acknowledge that fact later.

As a man, Jesus lived the most unique, yet most beautiful life, ever recorded. He was the kindest, most tender, most gentle, most patient, most sympathetic man that ever lived. He exuded love for every person He met. He hated to see people suffer. He loved to forgive. He loved to help. He wrought marvelous miracles to feed hungry people. While relieving the suffering, He frequently gave up eating for Himself. Multitudes of the weary, pain ridden and heartsick came to Him to find healing and relief. Yet Jesus was not a weak pushover, for He had no toleration for hypocrisy and sin. He dealt firmly with both underhanded religious leaders and His own disciples when they needed correction. It is said of Him, and of no other, that if all the deeds that He did were written, the world could not contain the books.

After revealing His character through His actions, Jesus completed the mission that He was sent to fulfill—He died on the cross to take away the sins of the world. He was always our Creator, He became our Redeemer and Savior.

It is because Christ demonstrated authority over death (by rising from the dead) that He is also our eternal hope. Christ is alive now. Jesus is not merely an historical character, but a living person. This is the most astounding historical fact of history and the most vital force in the world today. It is only because the Bible has been undermined from the very beginning (i.e., a recent creation has been

"CAUGHT HIM AT THE SCHOOL HANDING OUT BIBLES!"

replaced by evolution and billions of years) that the relevance of Jesus' life and death is also being ignored.

The whole Bible is built around this beautiful story of Christ and His promise of life eternal to those who accept Him. The Bible was written that we humans might believe, understand, know, love, and follow Christ. Christ is the center and heart of the Bible; the center and heart of history, and should be the center of our hearts and lives. Our eternal destiny is in His hand. Our acceptance or rejection of Him determines for each of us...eternal glory or eternal ruin... heaven or hell...one or the other.

We will all die physically but our spirit and soul are eternal, destined for either heaven or hell. We can bring nothing to heaven except those we have brought to Christ.

The most important decision everyone will make is, whether or not to acknowledge Jesus Christ as the Lord of their lives. Upon that decision depends everything. To accept Christ as Savior, Lord, and Master—to strive sincerely and devotedly to follow in the way of life which He taught—is by far the most reasonable and satisfying way to live. It brings peace of mind, contentment of heart, forgiveness, happiness, and hope. Devotion to Christ results in an abundant (but not trouble-free) life while here on earth and eternal life with God after death.

How can anyone choose to be so blind as to go through life and to face death without Christ? Apart from Christ, what is there, either for this world or the next, to make life worthwhile? Neither money, friends, power or possessions can bring lasting fulfillment. We can bring nothing to heaven except those we have brought to Christ. Everything else becomes irrelevant after our death and every one is destined to die. Every human being should welcome Christ with open arms and consider it the proudest privilege of their life to wear the Christian name. In order to gain admission to heaven, we only need to accept Jesus by faith as the Son of God and make Him our personal Lord and Savior. He is our Creator and Lord whether we are willing to acknowledge that fact or not. We can either willingly acknowledge Jesus as Lord of our lives now or, in sorrow, acknowledge that fact later. These are the terms of admission to heaven, acting on the first one leads to the others:

- **Implicit faith** in Jesus as Lord and Savior. This requires the admission that we are sinful and incapable of saving ourselves. We have to desire to make Jesus our Lord, rather than keeping ourselves as lord.
- **Inner cleansing** is then given to us upon our acceptance of Jesus as our Savior. No external correctness or works on our part can buy salvation.
- **Imitation** of His acts of loving service. This becomes our desire once we make Jesus our Lord and Savior. If we have no such desire, we need to examine our relationship with Him and question whether we are truly saved.

In the last analysis, the dearest, sweetest thing in life is the conscious realization that, in the inner depths of our motives, we live for Christ. Although our efforts are feeble compared to the power of our Creator, we must continue in our daily tasks with the hope of having done something of humble gratitude and adoration as an offering to the one who both made and saved us. We are told to be a *"living sacrifice."*[1] God desires nothing more than for us to spread the Gospel (good news) of His love to others. Jesus commanded Peter three times to, *"Feed my Sheep."*[2] We too should heed to this command.[3]

There is an excellent acronym for **BIBLE**—**B**e **I**nformed **B**efore **L**eaving **E**arth. The Bible must be central to our understanding of reality. As stated in the Gospel of John, *"In the beginning was the WORD and the WORD became flesh."* Jesus cannot be separated from the WORD of the Bible. As the Bible becomes irrelevant in people's minds and hearts, so too does Jesus Christ. This is why sinful mankind works so hard to undermine the Bible— starting with the very first chapters.

The *good news* is not merely that Jesus died for our sins according to the scriptures, but that he rose from the dead (1 Corinthians 15:3). The *even better news* is that He is also coming back very soon. We should live every day to His glory—expecting each day to be the day of His return. There are many who look to the Bible for indications of the time of His return. That time may be very close. According to the Word of God, we are to hold our hearts in readiness and live each day as if the Lord is keeping His appointment with destiny this very day. It is often asked when the Lord Jesus will return. My response is that it very well may be in the next instant of time (Matthew 24:42, Luke 21:36), *so be prepared*!

1. *Romans 12:1*
2. *John 21:15-17*
3. *Halley's Bible Handbook,* New Revised Edition, p.20-21

Chapter 5:
Creation is the Foundation

" Overwhelmingly strong proofs
of intelligent and benevolent
design lie all around us. The
atheistic idea is so nonsensical
that I cannot put it into words."

- Lord Kelvin

If salvation is so simple, why aren't more people accepting this free gift from God? Try to imagine yourself in the position of a person who has no background knowledge of Christianity. They did not grow up in a Christian home, never attended church, and have been indoctrinated in evolutionary concepts through our educational and media system. This person has been taught *against* Christianity by his/her parents, the media, teachers in school, museums, textbooks, and college professors. They have been taught that they cannot trust the Bible because it contradicts the "real world" and is full of ancient myths.

Imagine a Christian who meets this person and tells them there is a God of infinite love who made the world and cares for us. After this non-Christian listens, it wouldn't be surprising to hear him/her respond as follows, "I don't see any God of love. I see children suffering and dying. I see people killing and stealing. Disease and death seem to be everywhere. Nature is 'red in tooth and claw' as a poet once stated. It's a horrible world. I don't see your God of love. If your God does exist, He must be either too powerless to improve things or He is a sadistic ogre."

The non-Christian is looking at a fallen world, but they have been taught that the Fall is a myth. If they believe in God at all, they have been trained to believe that things were created by evolution to be the way they are. If

CREATIONWISE

GOD LOVES YOU AND HAS A WONDERFUL PLAN FOR YOUR LIFE!

©AIG 2003

Genesis is not literally true, then neither is Romans 8:22 when it states that: *"For we know that the whole creation groaneth and travaileth in pain together until now."*

When such a person is told about the God of creation, he subconsciously (and logically) blames God for the horrible condition of the world. After all, hasn't he been taught that God used evolution to make it this way?

Without an understanding of Genesis and the account of the Fall, he will not comprehend how there can be a God of love amidst the groaning. Even a Christian, when a loved one dies or some other tragedy strikes, cries out asking God why these things have to happen. Those who do not accept a literal six-day creation often blame God and become angry because they do not understand the real reason for death and suffering. In contrast to this, someone who understands creation as described in Genesis realizes that God is in control and that all things are being worked out for the good of those who love Him. Unfortunately, most Christians have been indoctrinated to believe that God "created" over billions of years, and that death, disease, and suffering are just part of God's creative process. But this is certainly not the God described in the Bible.

If we believe Genesis 1:31, then we realize that God created everything very good. So what happened to bring about this groaning world? It is vital that Christians understand what occurred in the universe as a result of Adam's fall into sin. The groaning, hurting world we now see around us (even though there is still a remnant of beauty from the original creation) exists because this is what *we* as human beings, brought upon ourselves.

In Colossians 1:17 and Hebrews 1:3, we learn that Jesus Christ, is the Creator of all things and upholds all things by the power of His Word. As John Gill has stated,

"The whole frame of nature would burst asunder and break in pieces, was it not held together by Him. Every created being has its support from Him, its consistence in Him; and all the affairs of Providence relating to all creatures are governed, directed, and managed by Him, in conjunction with the Father. The blessed Spirit preserves every creature in its being: supports it and supplies it with the necessities of life: rules and governs all, providentially orders and disposes of all things in the world, and that by His all-powerful will."

Several theories of modern physics, drawing on areas as diverse as quantum mechanics, relativity, and the electromagnetic theory of matter (*A Closer Look at the Evidence*—Feb. 5 and July 22) come to the conclusion that both matter and energy are just an energy simulation. We really don't even know what electrons and protons are; what keeps them moving, or what holds atoms together. The reason for our very existence, even at this very moment, is because God holds us together by His power. What an awesome thought! No wonder the Psalmist in Psalm 139 exclaimed, *"such knowledge is too wonderful for me. It is high, I cannot attain it."* [1]

God gave Adam a choice in the garden of Eden: choose God and His absolutes, or chose autonomy (i.e. make your own rules). Adam (we as rebellious creatures do the same thing) choose life without God. We did not want God's rules. We wanted to determine truth for ourselves. As a result, God, as a righteous judge, gave us, in a sense, what we wanted (and deserved). He has withdrawn some of His sustaining power and look what happened. Everything is running down and falling apart. We are now experiencing in our present world, a taste of what life would be like without God. This mess the world is in is entirely our fault.

In Deuteronomy 8:4; 29:5, and Nehemiah 9:21, we read how the Israelites, when they were in the wilderness for forty years, didn't see their clothes or shoes wear out. This was obviously a miracle of preservation from the Lord. Imagine, if God were to do this with everything in the entire universe, nothing would ever wear out. There would be no disease or suffering. This is what it was like in the Garden of Eden before the Fall and what it will be like on the new earth after the restoration.

Whenever people reject and suppress the undeniable evidence for God's existence (i.e. creation), He gives them over to their sinful desires.

In spite of our constant rebellion, God continues to be merciful to us. Even though we have a predisposition to want life without God, our Creator has given us only a taste of what this is like. He still upholds things so we can live in this world. The more God removes His restraining influence from the nations (it is God who raises up kings and destroys kingdoms), and the more we will see the horrible, sinful nature of man expressed in evil deeds.

We can see a dramatic example of this happening in America. This was once a great Christian nation. God's laws were respected and for the most part obeyed. But now we observe a nation full of fornication, wickedness, murder, deceit, haters of God, inventors of evil things, children disobedient to parents, and even the majority of churches which have compromised the Word of God with the teachings of sinful men. More and more people are rejecting the God of the Bible. Evolutionary teaching is rampant. We see a nation that seems to have lost a sense of right and wrong. There is a widespread denial of God's absolutes. America appears to have lost any absolute basis for morals. Other countries with a great Christian heritage (i.e., Europe) are even further down the slippery moral slope as they have totally accepted evolutionary *"myths"* as fact. As a direct consequence, Christianity has become irrelevant in these countries.

God has a warning for all nations. In the first chapter of Romans, we read that whenever people reject and suppress the undeniable evidence for God's existence, which can be seen through what he has made (creation), God gives them over to their sinful desires. *"[People] changed the truth of God into a lie, and worshipped and served the creature more than the Creator, who is blessed forever."*[2]

Worshipping the creation rather than acknowledging the Creator is an apt definition of evolution. This is essentially what Christians who compromise with evolution and add

THE STATE: ULTIMATE EARTHLY PROTECTOR OF LITTLE CHILDREN...

...WHO ARE BORN!

"millions of years" to Scripture's straightforward teachings are also doing—placing evolution (a bogus creative process) above the Creator (and His inspired Word). They have chosen to place the word of sinful, fallible people above God's Word—thus worshiping the creature (false prophets) rather than the Creator.[3]

Romans, chapter one, goes on to describe what happens when God withdraws even part of His restraining power. Things rapidly degenerate. *"And even as they did not like to retain God in their knowledge, God gave them over to a reprobate mind, to do those things which are not convenient: being filled with all unrighteousness, fornication, wickedness, covetousness, maliciousness: full of envy, murder, debate, deceit, malice, whisperers, backbiters, haters of God, despiteful, proud, boasters, inventors of evil things, disobedient to parents, without understanding, covenant-breakers, without natural affection, implacable, unmerciful: Who knowing the judgment of God, that they which commit such things are worthy of death, not only do the same, but have pleasure in them that do them."[4]*

This is exactly what has been happening in America over the last 100 years. May the warnings of Jerimiah and Isaiah be taken to heart by America's churches:

"Return, ye backsliding children, and I will heal your backslidings."[5]

"Let the wicked forsake his way, and the unrighteous man his thoughts: and let him return unto the LORD, and he will have mercy upon him; and to our God, for he will abundantly pardon."[6]

This following article is an example of the twisted backward thinking which results from people who have totally rejected the truth of the Bible and completely accepted their evolutionary education as a fact. This letter to the editor, by Harry Guth, was published in the Ocala, Florida **Star-Banner** on January 31, 2000, but similar letters can be found written to the editors of any newspaper in America:

Holy Hokum!

"How many readers are aware of the Pisonian Conspiracy Theory? After watching the Republican debates recently and hearing of a presidential Candidate say, 'Jesus changed my life,' there needs to be an examination of these people running for the office of president. The subject of whether or not Jesus of the New Testament actually existed needs to be tested. No! He, it, or whatever, did not exist in reality. He was the invention of myth.

There is conclusive proof, with facts, dates, and historical details, that Jesus was a deliberate fabrication and design of Arius Calpurnius Piso - Pen name - 'Flavius Josephus'. The fact that a physical being cannot be born - conceived - through the intervention of a ghost, angel, or a God, is all the proof necessary to positively dispute any Christian babble that such a character ever existed as a reality. Until there is scientific evidence - an improbability - that can be established beyond all doubt that the supernatural existence of a God is probable, all frivolous claims for the existence of Jesus are superficial, fantastic proclamations of Holy Hokum *and theological bunk.*

We do not need a 'Jesus Freak' in the White House. These people are psychotic, and least of all we don't need candidates telling us how righteous they are because Jesus has saved them. No one needs saving because no one is lost!

Elect one of these 'Freaks' to the White House and the next thing you'll find them saying, 'Behold, I am your promised Messiah!' When religion ruled the world it was the Dark Ages. Einstein once told Neil's Bohr, 'God does not play dice with the universe,' neither do we need politicians perpetuating the Jesus myth."

The reason we have judges removing the Ten Commandments from public view and stating that the Pledge of Allegiance is unconstitutional is because the recognition of the Bible as Truth has been eroded. Imagine everyone in Washington setting their own rules without any thought about God or absolute truth. Many believe that we are close to that situation today. Will anarchy eventually result? Will we will have another Nero, Hitler or Stalin rise to power in order to "restore order." If so, they will merely be dictating their own philosophy upon us.

God has blessed this country with the freedom to pick godly leaders who acknowledge the Bible as the only true source of moral authority. Every Christian should exercise his right to vote at our elections so that we may slow the erosion of our freedoms which are being replaced by dictator-like arbitrary laws. Make your Christian voice heard by voting for leaders who demonstrate through their actions that they respect the authority of the Bible. Write letters to the editor exposing the lies of evolution. Start a creation column in your church newsletter. The resources at the back of this book are designed to help you make a difference and to turn the tide that is overwhelming our churches and our country.

1. *Psalm 139:6*
2. *Romans 1:25*
3. *Answers in Genesis Update*, April 1999, Vol 6, #3.
4. *Romans 1:28-32*
5. *Jerimiah 3:22*
6. *Isaiah 55:7*

Chapter 6:
Conclusion

" The whole reason that we have missing links is because...they are missing."

-Ken Ham

The wisest man to have ever lived , King Solomon, wrote the books of Proverbs and Ecclesiastes. In one section Solomon lists seven things which the Lord hates[1]:

- A lying tongue
- A haughty look
- Hands that shed innocent blood
- A heart that weaves wicked thoughts
- Feet that hurry to do evil
- A false witness who lies with every breath
- A person that sows dissension

Notice that three of the seven sins are directly related to lies (a lying tongue, a false witness, and a haughty look—*which is a lie of self deception*). The greatest lie of the twentieth century is the deception that we are here as a result of random mutations and that the earth is billions of years old. The lie of evolution has lead countless millions of people away from a closer relationship with the Lord and it is long overdo for the Christian Church to expose this lie for what it is.

We will close this book by looking at how creation is typically presented in churches. Most Sunday School/ Christian school literature concentrates on teaching Bible stories. The problem is that the teaching rarely goes beyond the stories and their *spiritual* applications. We teach about the days of creation but never tie creation to biology. We teach about Noah and the Flood but ignore the implications of this Flood on the geology of our planet. We teach about Jonah and the whale, Jesus' death and resurrection; the feeding of the five thousand, but we fail to drive home that these miraculous events do not contradict science because we never mention science and how it works. It is almost as if the Church is afraid to relate the

Bible to the *physical* world around us. So we stop at "telling Bible stories." Then the children go into the world for thousands of hours of evolutionary indoctrination by public schools, secular television, newspapers and magazines.

And what is the world teaching them? That they can't trust the Bible. That science has proved the Bible wrong. That Noah couldn't get all the animals into the ark, it's just a fairy tale. That dinosaurs prove evolution is true. That humans evolved from "ape-men." That the story of Adam and Eve is a fairy tale. That there's no evidence of God's existence. And besides, Christians can't answer simple

THE BIBLE IS NOT TRUE! THESE ROCK LAYERS SHOW THAT THE EARTH IS MILLIONS OF YEARS OLD! YOU HAVE TO BELIEVE ME! I AM A SCIENTIST!

MILLIONS OF YEARS

ROCK LAYERS

I'LL JUST ACCEPT THE MILLIONS OF YEARS AND ADD IT TO THE BIBLE!

Scientist

Theologian

Used by permission of AiG - www.AnswersinGenesis.org

questions like, "Where did Cain get his wife?" In short, they are taught that they can't trust God's Word.

And how do most churches respond to this barrage of anti-Christian propaganda? *They just keep teaching Bible stories.* The result is totally predictable—kids are walking away from the church in droves because it isn't relevant to the "real world." These churches aren't dealing with the real attack on Christianity which is the undermining of the authority of Scripture. They don't know what to do about the collapsing Christian culture because they have quit defending the basis upon which Christianity stands—the literal authority of the Bible. They see the symptoms of the rejection of biblical authority—abortion, homosexuality, euthanasia, divorce, pornography, etc.—but not the foundational problem. They have abandoned the foundation from their thinking by not emphasizing the reality of the first eleven chapters of Genesis. Christians need to be trained to believe and defend God's word from Genesis to Revelation. The resources from *Search for the Truth Ministries* can help you and others to do just that.

Most people in our churches don't understand that the Bible is a *true history book.* Christianity is not based on myths or interesting stories, it is based on real history. There was a real Adam to whom we are all related. There was a real Garden of Eden and a real event called the Fall, which is why we are all sinners. There is a real curse, which is why there is death and suffering.

As we look through the pages of church history, we find that the church has had many periods of decline (such as the dark ages and crusades) and expansion (like the Reformation). Another reformation is desperately needed. The Church needs to return to believing the first eleven chapters of Genesis and acting on that belief. *Belief without action is dead.*

Given the proliferation of false religions, the distortions of the Gospel, and the moral and spiritual decline in the West, it seems like the purpose of God is failing in the world. To conclude this would require a profound misunderstanding of divine providence. *Nothing* is happening which God has not anticipated and *nothing* is happening in the world which is not a part of His *divine plan*. The purposes of God are on track and we have been called to be a part of His plan to bring the truth to our generation. The darker things look, the brighter the light of truth as it shines for those who are not too spiritually blind to see the truth. Ultimate, eternal success is inevitable. The Church has suffered through persecution, innumerable heresies, division and failure. Yet through it all, and in spite of human failure, God's plan has and will always be accomplished.[1,2]

The challenge for us is to deepen our understanding of *the truth*, *our commitment to it*, and *share the truth* with others. Since we can only take people as far as we ourselves have gone, it is important that we grow in our own discipleship and knowledge of Jesus; teaching as Christ commanded us in Matthew 28:19-20: *"Go ye therefore, and teach all nations, baptizing them in the name of the Father, and of the Son, and of the Holy Ghost:* **teaching them to observe all things** *whatsoever I have commanded you; and lo, I am with you always, even unto the end of the world."*

AMEN

1. *Why Won't They Listen: Creation Evangelism For The New Millennium*, Ken Ham
2. *Christ Among Other Gods*, Erwin W.Lutzer

About the Authors

John Filippi is a Christian who attends the Evangelical Lutheran Church of America (ELCA). John worked as a design engineer for Chrysler Corporation for 31 years before retiring in Dunnellon, Florida with his wife Vivian. It is John's passion to see the ELCA—and all of America's Christian Churches—return to the rock solid Word of God as the final authority on matters of faith, morality, and reality. The Filippi's have nine children, twenty two grand children, and five great grand children and they hope this book will be a legacy for future generations.

Bruce Malone works as a research leader for the Dow Chemical Company. Mr. Malone has a B.S. in Chemical Engineering from the University of Cincinnati and holds 18 patents for Dow Chemical. Bruce is interested in every aspect of science and biblical studies and has been teaching on the harmony of the evidence between creation and science for over 15 years. Bruce lives in Midland, Michigan, with his wife Robin and their four children—Michael, Marc, Margaret, and Matthew. *Search for the Truth Publications* was started to distribute interesting and affordable books on the evidence and relevance of creation.

Enjoy the Illustrations?

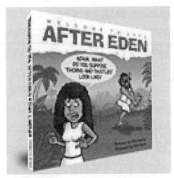

The best of Dan Lietha's hilarious, thought-provoking After Eden cartoons, collected for the first time in one book!

Get the entire collection!

Order today at Answersingenesis.org

- -

Creation Magazine

Keep your family informed on the latest easy-to-understand evidences for creation. This unique full-color family magazine gives God the glory, refutes evolution, and gives you the answers to defend your faith. It contains exciting articles and great witnessing material you won't find anywhere else. Each issue includes a beautifully illustrated full-color children's section. Powerful ammunition to intelligently discuss nature, history, science, the Bible, and related subjects. Delivered to your home every three months.

Order today at Answersingenesis.org

Over 70% of churched youth walk away from their faith in the first year of college.

WHY?

Because they do not understand how the Bible is relevant to the world around them nor do they know the evidence that makes the Bible the most credible book on Earth.

TRUTH MATTERS!

Give every youth the tools they need to trust His Word.

Put *Search for the Truth* resources to use!

- A perfect youth group graduation gift.
- Affordable resources to help make sharing God's Truth easy.
- Build confidence in having a "ready answer" in defense of your faith.
- Help "wake-up" our churches by bringing His Word alive.
- Use in Sunday School classes, Bible studies, schools.
- Permission is granted to reprint all materials.

See *Search for the Truth* resources at:

- SearchfortheTruth.net
- Amazon.com
- Answersingenesis.org

America is losing its Christian heritage!

§ Prayer and Bibles have been removed from schools.

§ Reminders of Christ at Christmas are outlawed.

§ The public display of the Ten Commandments is banned.

§ The sanctity of marriage is under attack.

All because the Bible has been undermined as the source of truth and reality.

- A daily devotional with an evidence for the existence of our Creator for every day of the year!
- 408 pages of unique and fascinating evidence for the trustworthiness of the Bible from 26 subject areas and over 70 expert sources.
- Anyone from elementary age to adult will love this book on the wonders of God's creation.

- The story of what happens when the evidence for creation is placed into public newspapers.
- Individual articles cover every aspect of the evidence for creation — for junior high to adult ages.
- This highly enjoyable 144 page book is extensively illustrated for easy reading and reproduction.

- We are removing Christian influences from every public corner. What is happening to America?
- Understand what is at the root of the battle for our culture and what you can do about it.
- An overview of the truth and relevance of the Bible — a must read for every Christian.

To order these resources send a check and this order form to:

Search for the Truth
3275 E. Monroe Road
Midland, MI 48642
or call:
989.837.5546

All books (mix & match for the lowest cost):

Buy More for Less!

1 copy @ $12.00 each

2 - 9 copies @ $9.00 each

10 or more copies @ $6.00 each

(Shipping & handling is included in the cost.)

- - - - - - - - - - - - - - - - - - - -

ITEM	NUMBER ORDERED	COST EACH	TOTAL
A Closer Look at the Evidence			
Seach for the Truth			
By His Word			
Search for the Truth (Video)		$10.00	
Why are we losing our Culture (audio)		$ 3.00	
Call for even lower case quantity pricing!		**Subtotal**	
	MI Residents add 6% sales tax		
	Total enclosed by check		

SHIP TO:

Name: _____

Address: _____

City/State/Zip: _____

Phone: _____

E-mail: _____